Knowledge Management-

Volume 4:

Knowledge and Innovation

Jon-Arild Johannessen

Copyright © 2016 Jon-Arild Johannessen

All rights reserved.

ISBN-13:
978-1537507040

ISBN-10:
1537507044

DEDICATION

To my wife

CONTENTS

DEDICATION iii

CONTENTS iv

ACKNOWLEDGMENTS vi

Chapter 1 Knowledge management and innovation theory 8
  Introduction 8
  VISION 13
  KNOWLEDGE-CREATION 17
    Systemic-knowledge 26
    Explicit knowledge 27
    Tacit knowledge 27
    Hidden knowledge 28
    Relationship knowledge 29
  KNOWLEDGE- INTEGRATION-AND USE 30
  ORGANIZATIONAL INNOVATION 34
  Conclusion 37
    Practical implications 37
    Theoretical implications 38
    References 42

CHAPTER 2 High-tech value creation 58
  Introduction 58
    The development of new expertise 62
    Global clusters of expertise 69
    The global market 79
  Conclusion 89
    Theoretical consequences for individuals and organisations 89
    Practical implications for leaders and organisations 94
  References 96

Chapter 3 Systemic Thinking, Knowledge and organizational innovations 103

Introduction	103
Normative open and cognitive closed	108
The normative superstructure and the normatively closed loop	118
Information capital	127
The cognitively open loop.	132
Problem definition	137
Framing the situation	142
The learning loop and tacit knowledge	143
Conclusion	152
References	158
Chapter on concepts	**167**
Index	**204**
ABOUT THE AUTHOR	**209**

Jon-Arild Johannessen

ACKNOWLEDGMENTS

I want to thank my students at Bachelor, Master and Ph.D. level, for useful comments

Chapter 1 Knowledge management and innovation theory

Introduction

" Increasingly,--, developing and managing human intellect and skills, more than managing and deploying physical and capital assets, will be the dominant concern of managers in successful companies" (Quinn, 1992: 439). The question is how? This is the question which constitutes this chapter. The purpose is to develop some rudiments of innovation theory based upon vision, knowledge creation and knowledge-integration- and use, collectively constituting what is here named knowledge management.

People at work need a vision, a sense of purpose on meaning transcending the trivia of everyday efforts (Vleck & Davidson, 1992). Organizations must be infused with vision, similar to the way institutions are infused with value, in order to be effective in the hypercompetitive environment (Divine, 1994), or turbo economy. Hypercompetition, i.e. when the changes in the environment is so fast that the system has not recovered from one change before a new change enter the system, is a new reality and we need new ways of dealing with this reality.

In order to share vision, communication is essential. Communication is the sum total of verbal and non verbal communication, with or without the use of information and communication technology. It may or may not stand at the top, but it will always be a strategic responsibility to create and maintain visions to provide leadership functions in the turbo economy, or with Quinn (1992: 375): "At the very top, creating and driving a consistent vision of the company's or group's purpose is the primary skill that provides the glue for all its highly disaggregated units".

Managers are vigorously, even ruthlessly, paring down the mix of activities and the number of employees within their companies, to catch up with the hypercompetition they are faced with. The buzz words are "lean production" (Womack et.al., 1990), "cross-functional teams" (Parker, 1994), "business process reengineering"(Hammer and Champy, 1993), "The Connected Corporation" (Lewis, 1995), "core competencies" (Hamel & Prahlad,1994) etc. This has led to entrepreneurialism (Peters, 1987), a more clearly defined accountability, agility organizations, the moving of decision-making closer to the customer and the removing of management layers (Schaaf, 1995; Prahald & Hamel, 1996). In this transition the focus on knowledge as a productive resource for innovation, economic growth and survival, in addition to the productivity of the knowledge workers, has received increasing attention during the

90s. The persons who have discussed this theme extensively have been, among others, Toffler (1990), Reich (1991), Quinn (1992), Drucker (1993), Archibagi & Michie (1995), Lundvall (1992), Lundvall & Johnson (1994), Divine (1994) in addition to Nonaka & Takeuchi (1995) and Leonard-Barton (1995). Innovation in this context will be seen as the heart of productivity (Fruin, 1997, Solow, 1997), and the positioning of companies in an increasingly internationalized and globalized turbo-economy (Freeman, 1995; Landabaso, 1995). In the new perspectives it is in particular technological changes, interactive learning, knowledge development, knowledge integration and practical application of knowledge which are the focal elements (Grant, 1996, Fruin, 1997, Stewart, 1997, Sveiby, 1997).

Archibugi and Michie (1995) argue that contemporary economic systems have become more "knowledge-intensive" than in the past. Knowledge intensive companies are described by Sveiby (1997:19) in the following way:»Most employees of knowledge companies are highly qualified educated professionals-that is they are knowledge workers. Their work consists largely of converting information to knowledge, using their own competencies for the most part, sometimes with the assistance of suppliers of information or specialized knowledge. These companies have few tangible assets. Their intangible assets are much more valuable than their tangible assets». But still says Fruin (1997:17):»Western management is mostly concerned with efficient use of tangible resources---. These are things that can be counted, routinely depreciated, and easily valued; balance sheets where people are a residual resource, not a core one». In the knowledge-intensive companies knowledge workers, however, prefer performance oriented methods (Sadler, 1988) and/or task driven organisation of work processes (Beer et.al., 1990).

Continuous changes in the state of knowledge produce new disequilibrium situations and, therefore, new profit opportunities (Jacobsen, 1992), and they do so at an increasing pace. Unfortunately for many companies, so does imitation, creating a dynamic competitive process. Thus, as the competitive process eliminates an opportunity, changes in the stream of knowledge produce other opportunities. This is in line with Schumpeters vision of competition as "a process of creative destruction", rather than as a static equilibrium condition (Mahoney and Pandian, 1992). Consequently, there is an increasing emphasis on a knowledge-based economy (Quinn, 1992; Drucker, 1993, Nonaka & Takeuchi, 1995; Barton, 1995). This unending stream of knowledge keeping market in perpetual motion, calls for companies to execute continous improvements and continuous innovation, while simultaneously limiting imitation.

Certain firms have more information than others, and turning this into knowledge gives them an advantage in ascertaining market inefficiencies, putting them in a better position to innovate. "Innovation, that is the application of knowledge to produce new knowledge.---It requires systematic efforts, and a high degree of organization" (Drucker, 1993: 173). Thus, as we enter the knowledge society, ownership of knowledge and information, as a source of competitive advantage, is becoming increasingly important. However, information is only the raw material; knowledge upon which action is based, is the value-added and in the knowledge based company, and the value added comes from the members of the organization. This is also emphasized of the so-called "new growth theory" (Scott, 1989), and the resource-based view (Reed & De Fillippi, 1990; Barney, 1991; Black & Boal, 1994; Collis & Montgomery, 1995). This is also a main core in the knowledge-based theory of the firm (Grant, 1996).

The model upon which this chapter is based is shown in fig. 1

Fig. 1 organizational innovation

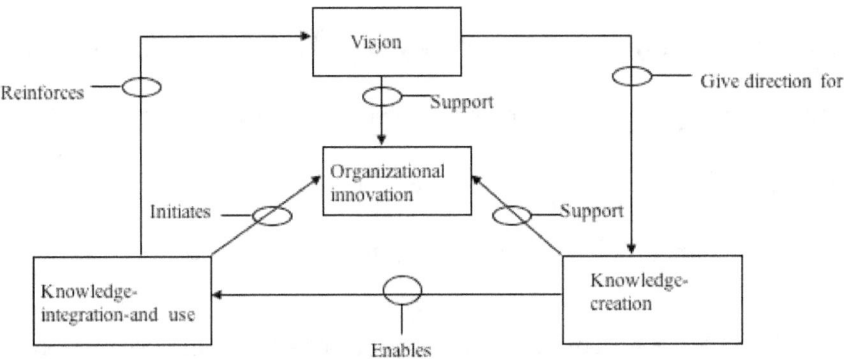

The chapter is organized as follows: First we discuss vision. Then we elaborate on knowledge creation. Thirdly, we discuss knowledge-integration and -use. We will then integrate the chapter by discussing organizational innovation. In the conclusion we will propose aspects of a theory, i.e. systems of propositions, for organizational innovation based on information-and knowledge-management.

VISION

A critical issue facing companies today, is how to manage an unpredictable and unstable future. Since the future is basically unpredictable, evoking images, rather than established facts, will serve as our main guidance when venturing into the unknown. The more unpredictable and uncertain the world is, the more companies must rely on creative initiatives from the employees to be able to create the desired future (Thurow, 1996). There is no crystal ball which companies may use to look into the future, but there are creative ways in which they can help bring it about by actively pursuing their visions.

It is the tension between the actual performance of the organization, and the desired future expressed through a clear and unambiguous vision, which is often referred to as the vision led company (Kanter et.al., 1992). It is this tension between actuality and potentiality which Senge (1990:150) refers to as creative tension. But with vision we also have bounded vision, expressed by Fransman (1990: 3):"---the field of vision of for-profit corporations is determined largely by their existing activities in factor and product markets, in production and in R&D,---. The resulting bounded vision implies that new technologies emerging from neighboring areas where the corporation does not have current activities are likely to take some time to penetrate the corporations field of vision.---. In view of their bounded vision, corporations often tend to underinvest in the creation of such technology". Bounded vision limits the strategic window of an organization, filtering information, which should not be filtered, and directing the knowledge creation process of the system, often in a non-consciously way. In this way vision in organizations function as a sort of autopoietic system (Luhman, 1986, 1992), i.e. it reproduces the existing knowledge structures in the system, with little cognitive openness to other knowledge structures in the environment (Johannessen, 1998).

To speed up the innovation process the firm should make extensive contacts with different institutions to help them overcome the bounded vision, i.e. participating in external meetings and using electronic media to get in contact with people outside the organization (Brynjolfsson, 1994; brynjolfsson & Hitt, 1996). This would increase sensitivity to change and bring in a proactive (Ackoff, 1981) attitude in the organization. Bounded vision may also be seen as a type of firm-specific hidden knowledge, i.e. the disposition to think and act which rests in the routines of the organization, hindering the organizations ability to cope in the turbo-economy (Johannessen, 1998).

The vision is meant to generate a clear purpose, i.e. what makes us distinctive, and to bring forth the necessary change in the organization to achieve the desired future goals (Kanter et.al., 1992). Therefore, the communication of the vision becomes a central point in organizational innovation. The vision gives identity to the firm, it separates the system from competitors, integrates and co-ordinate the strategy to a functional whole, or as Fruin (1997: 24) puts it; in the knowledge-intensive firm: «A unified strategy, structure, and culture culminating in a single firms strategic vision holds everything together».

Vision has to do with a proactive attitude (Kanter, 1986). In management literature, this has, among other things, been pointed out by Ackoff (1981, 1984), in his "Creating the Corporate Future" concept, and Weick's (1979) concept of "Future Perfect Thinking". Kanter et. al. (1992:383) state that the "vision is an attempt to articulate what a desired future for a company would be". Vision, understood in this way, can help the organizations to innovate and keep up with forces in the hypercompetitive environment.

The purpose of the vision is thus to take advantage of the creative tension between actuality and potentiality by creating a foresight both for the members of the organization and the targeted customers, in order to generate the necessary change in the organization.

Rules and routines have a tendency to be preferred to vision (Kanter, 1983: 304). To make the vision influential on routines and rules, the whole pattern of connections, which the routines and rules are part of, must be revealed (Whipp et.al., 1987; Whipp & Pettigrew, 1993). This implies that the visionary leader must "operate at levels of patterns of change as well as events" (Senge, 1990: 355).

Vision is here seen as a visualization of a metaphor, a symbol or a dream. Through a direct connection between mission and vision, a more active participation from the employees could be achieved. Consequently, the mission is closely related to the purpose of our life and work. It is what we have to do, why we are doing it, and what we seek to achieve when performing actions connecting vision and mission.

The purpose of linking vision and mission is to make the employees part of something which will motivate them to view their daily work in a larger context, making them encouraged by the purpose of their work, both during and after the process. A clear vision integrates the entities in the organization combining the different activities of the business and gives direction for future actions.

KNOWLEDGE-CREATION

There is a world wide agreement that knowledge and innovation is the competitive strength needed for successful companies (Nonaka,1991; Nonaka & Takeuchi,1995; European Commission, 1995; Fruin, 1997; Thurow, 1996; Stewart, 1997; Sveiby, 1997). Nobel prize winner Simon

Kuznets (1966: 6) puts it this way:» an increase in the stock of useful knowledge and the extension of its application are of the essence of modern economic growth».

We see the capital-intensive and labor-intensive organization of the past, the emergence of the knowledge and service intensive organization, a firm which employs a high percentage of qualified manpower (Fruin, 1997). Therefore, in contrast to the organization of yesterday, where the major source of control relative to the firm was located externally (Prahalad & Hamel, 1994: 7), i.e. the IO-paradigm of strategy, we see the emergence of a new and major source of control, which is internal (Prahalad & Hamel, 1996), i.e. the resource-based view with its emphasize on invisible assets.

Invisible assets (Itami & Roehl, 1987) are the unobserved factors creating knowledge in the organization. The organizations that will excel in the years to come will be the ones understanding how to gain the commitment of employees at all levels and continually expand their capacity to learn (Senge, 1990). A presupposition is, however, that a helping attitude penetrates the whole organisation, because this is an important factor gaining competitive advantage in the knowledge-intensive firm (Heimer, 1992).

In the knowledge-based company, the value added for the customers comes from the communication among the members of the organization (Howells, 1996). This could be done by building virtual team-networks, i.e. intranet, extranet, value added on net etc.(Evans & Wurster, 1997), to help ideas flowing and create new knowledge, thus building relationship-knowledge. Relationship knowledge is really about getting new personal contacts and serve old ones, both internally, e.g. peers, firm representatives, subordinates etc., and externally, e.g. customers, suppliers, government representatives etc.

The degree of creativity decides whether information is changed into knowledge, upon which action is based. The important track in a knowledge-based company will be to move from imagination to motivation, to planning, to action and further to evaluation, satisfaction, and realization (Thurow, 1996). This demands creativity, vision, knowledge creation and organizational learning.

In the 1980s the strategy perspective for the large corporations was based on decisions to invest, divest and make businesses grow. These strategies were conceived and executed by a few people at the top of the organization (Mintzberg, 1978; 1983; 1987; 1989, Ackoff, 1981). It was a combination of economics of scale, top down management, and specialization (Mintzberg, 1979; Thurow, 1996). The challenge of the future will depend upon the involvement of the many, for speed, quality, innovation, customer-focus and productivity (Sveiby, 1997, Stehr, 1994, Stewart, 1997), to make relationship-knowledge an important factor for competitive advantage. It evokes images of a well-integrated organization where understanding of the challenges in the marketplace is widely understood and provides the context in which decisions can be made at all levels in the organization(Quinn, 1992, Drucker, 1993).

Leonard-Barton (1995: 8) says:" knowledge building for an organization occurs by combining peoples distinct individualities with a particular set of activities". This presupposes that interactive learning can take place in the system. The importance of interactive learning in companies has been discussed by Teece (1986; 1988), among others. Tushman & Nadler (1986: 75) explicitly point out that innovative organizations have one thing in common; they are: "highly effective learning systems." To achieve this, an organization aimed at "both stability and change" (Tushman & Nadler, 1986: 75) is required, which means that the relationships between the actors is important, and also the system-environment relationships.

Participation and organizational learning actually demand that the middle managers or the project leaders (or both) take risks. These are also the lessons learnt from Japan which Nonaka & Takeuchi (1995: 233) teach us: "---in our view, middle managers play a key role in the organizational knowledge-creation process." They continue, however, "---in the West, --- middle managers have been portrayed as "cancer" and a "disappearing breed". In contrast, in a knowledge-creating company middle managers are positioned as the "knot", "bridge" and "knowledge engineers", because they are key holders of relationship-knowledge.

Tacit knowledge[1] (Polanyi, 1962) creating invisible assets is skill-based and people-intensive (Hart, 1995). This implies that as a resource, people are important, not just as participants in the labor force, but as accumulators and producers of invisible assets (Itami & Roehl, 1987; Bonoma, 1985; Reed & DeFillippi, 1990, McGrath et. al., 1995). This is also in line with Jacobsen (1992) who argues that invisible assets are key success factors because they are difficult to obtain, and Itami & Roehl (1987) who argue that invisible assets often are the only source of competitive edge that can be sustained over time. Also Nonaka & Takeuchi (1995) emphasize tacit knowledge as a main source creating

---

[1] Tacit knowledge is linked to experience, action and concrete contexts. Tacit knowledge is difficult to formulate in words, therby making it available for the computer. Tacit knowledge is interwoven in a tradition which the actors is part of (Nonaka, 1994).

new knowledge and continuous innovation. Tacit knowledge is the practical knowledge used to perform a task, and it is also «the knowledge that is used as a tool to handle what is being focused on» (Sveiby, 1997: 30). Consequently, tacit knowledge is in the business context: practical, action oriented, experience-based, contextual linked and personal, but not subjective or relative. It is objective, i.e. empirically testable and checkable, in the sense that it is objective in its consequences. This means that the work done by the use of tacit knowledge can be tested for quality, durability, reliability and to the reductions in the cost of production. Tacit knowledge is as real as explicit knowledge, but the processes to get this kind of knowledge, i.e. tacit knowing, rely on awareness of details we can't specify or test in any scientific way. But this does not hold for tacit knowledge, which is the outcome of the processes of tacit knowing. Tacit knowing is a process of a complex whole, a pattern which escape when taken apart for analysis. But tacit knowing is not only involved in the process by which tacit knowledge is gained. It is also involved in the processes by which all knowledge is gained (Polanyi, 1958: 49-69). For Polanyi (1958) tacit knowing is the dominant principle of all knowledge.

Lundvall (1995) says:" Perhaps it is not at all fruitful to regard tacit versus codified knowledge as two different pools where there is a flow from one to the other. The relationships are much more complex and symbiotic". This is also emphasized by Nonaka (1991, 1994) and Nonaka & Takeuchi (1995), and is also a main point by Polanyi (1958, 1962, 1966). Our contribution to this debate is the following statement: Tacit knowledge is objective in the sense that it is objective in its consequences, i.e. empirically testable.

An example of a successful company, where the active use of tacit knowledge on the part of companies has generated performance and innovation in Scandinavia, is the Swedish company Ramnæs (Laestadius, 1996). Their knowledge basis is tacit, and: "Largely acquired through on-the -job and organizational learning» (Eliason, 1996:179).

As a result of the more complex nature of work and the turbo-economy, the composition of the workforce will shift away from employees who have a traditional, practical training background and towards an ever increasing number of employees who have had a higher education and are theoretically well equipped (Quinn et. al., 1996). This type of employee must possess methodological strength, be capable of working in a problem definition and problem-oriented manner and possess skills for both analysis and synthesis. Nonaka & Takeuchi (1995: 237) says about this:"---the essence of knowledge creation is deeply rooted in the process of building and managing synthesis", i.e. our dispositions to think and act, what we here denote as hidden knowledge..

However, also the ability to innovate and willingness to run risks will be in demand. Leonard-Barton (1995:75) refers to this type of knowledge as T-shaped skills. The persons possessing this type of knowledge have a combination of theoretical and practical knowledge, and simultaneously have the ability to see how their branch of knowledge interacts with other branches of knowledge to function as a whole. These are persons with systemic knowledge, who understand the language of all branches, as a contrast to branch knowledge (Iansiti, 1993:193). These persons have usually expanded their competence across several functional branch areas, and thus developed the skills of systemic thinking (Johannessen, 1996, 1997). For the organization organizing knowledge in a systemic way will mean to let the knowledge worker be dependent on another knowledge workers specialist knowledge, and the technologies in the system as a whole, too make use of his own knowledge.

Based on the above discussion we will propose a typology of knowledge, which could be used for knowledge creation and knowledge integration aimed at innovation, which is shown in fig. 3 later in the chapter.

The distinctions in the figure below (fig. 2) is knowledge which is easily communicated to others, and knowledge which is difficult to communicate to others. A distinction of this type can be detected with Polanyi (1962), Quinn et. al. (1996) and Winter (1987). The other distinction is knowledge which is attainable and comprehensive, and knowledge which is attainable but difficult to comprehend. A distinction of this type can be detected with Polanyi (1958) and Innis (1994).

Fig. 2 A typology of knowledge

	Attainable and comprehensive	Attainable but difficult to comprehend
Relatively easy to communicate	Explicit knowledge	Systemic-knowledge
Difficult to communicate	Relationship-knowledge	Tacit knowledge and hidden knowledge

As a basic rule all knowledge (in figure 2) is mutually complementary and not reciprocally preclusive.

Systemic-knowledge

Systemic-knowledge is a sort of knowing how we know, i.e. the patterns which combine. Systemic- knowledge is both a process and a product. As a process it is expressed by Maturana & Varela (1987:24): "Reflection is a process of knowing how we know". As a product it is knowledge on how we think. Systemic-knowledge has bearing on the perspectives of individuals, i.e. what is seen and how this is perceived. The perspective generates meaning in terms of how the work is perceived and interpreted, in addition to adding input as to what a person is looking for in a job context. Systemic-knowledge is thus a form of split interpretation competence among the persons sharing the perspective. In this way systemic-knowledge directly influences these persons as to what type of explicit knowledge is relevant and meaningful for the company. The more uniform this perspective is among the most important actors of the company, the more influential this perspective will be as to what knowledge type (e.g. explicit versus tacit) is critical to the competitive position of the company. The persons in the company who have various degree of systemic-knowledge or different basis perspectives, will be able to view the same phenomenon, but interpret it differently, giving it various meanings relative to the opportunities and challenges of the company (Knorr-Cetina, 1981; Czarniawska-Joerges, 1992).

Explicit knowledge

Explicit knowledge is the part of our knowledge base which can be easily communicated to others as information, i.e. know what. Explicit knowledge involves knowing facts (Sveiby, 1975: 35). Explicit knowledge can be objective and intersubjective. Bunge (1983: 80) defines objective knowledge in the following way: "Let p be a piece of explicit knowledge. Then p is objective if and only if a) p is public (intersubjective) in some society, and b) p is testable (checkable) either conceptually or empirically".

Tacit knowledge

Tacit knowledge (Polanyi, 1962) is a form of skill, ability or "techne", i.e. know how, which is difficult to communicate to other as information, but:" much of what Michael Polanyi has called tacit knowledge is expressible- in so far as it is expressible at all-in metaphor" (Nisbet,

1969: 5). Drucker (1993: 24), says about tacit knowledge: "the only way to learn techne was through apprenticeship and experience". David & Foray (1995) also stresses that no knowledge is tacit by nature, what has to be done is to create incentives to make tacit knowledge communicable. Polanyi (1962: 54) says that this sort of knowledge also can be regarded as connoisseurship, and his example is the good wine-taster.

Tacit knowledge is embedded in the praxical matrix and it express itself through practical knowledge, reflected over time through experience in the same context. The praxical matrix is interwoven to a pattern which combine tacit knowledge to action, i.e. the integration and indwelling of experience with formal knowledge, so it is attainable but not easily comprehensible.

Hidden knowledge

Hidden knowledge, is the premises, prerequisites and motives influencing our disposition to- think and- act. Hidden knowledge influences the way we think and act, as a sort of personal paradigm, or the technical-economic paradigm in the business world, a trajectory which leads our way of thinking and acting when expressing and interpreting, among other things, new ideas. Hidden knowledge organizes the development of mental models, the nature of the abstraction we make, the choice of variables, problems or phenomena, the facts we choose to focus on, our underlying metaphysical positions, our theoretical "tastes" etc. Hidden knowledge can be divided in two parts: disposition to think and disposition to act. In this way hidden knowledge is linked to company-specific norms. We find support for the concept "hidden knowledge" in Schutz' (1990, Vol. 1 and 2) "epoche" concept.

Relationship knowledge

Relationship knowledge, i.e. know who, :"involves the social capability to establish relationships to specialized groups in order to draw upon their expertise" (Lundvall, 1995). In a time where turbulence, change and hypercompetition, are accelerating it is crucial for organizational survival to invest in relationship knowledge. Part of the relationship knowledge remain intact in codified knowledge, such as the name of the organization, the image of the organization in the marked, customer registers, software manuals, and so on (Sveiby, 1997). The type of relationship knowledge which is relatively easy to communicate, may be classified as explicit knowledge.

KNOWLEDGE- INTEGRATION-AND USE

Knowledge which is easily communicated to others are learned and shared in the formal education system an in the business world. We are so good at it in the West, that we have "forgotten" knowledge which is not easily communicated to others (Sveiby, 1997, Stewart, 1997, Howells, 1996). Howells (1996: 91) says: «Just as technological innovation up to the 1960´s was treated as an unexplained variance in economic growth and performance, so tacit knowledge as an element within technological innovation has, until recently, been seen in a similar way». But, as shown by Nonaka and Takeuchi (1995), this knowledge may be how Japanese companies create the dynamics of continuos improvement and continuos innovation, and is no «recognized as playing a key role in firm growth and economic competitiveness» (Howells, 1996: 91).

The emphasis on tacit knowledge as a strategic competitive factor is linked to the globalization of the economy (Thurow, 1997) and hypercompetition (D´aveni, 1994) in the marked.

Tacit knowledge is learned by using, doing and experimenting. It need to become explicit: «otherwise it cannot be examined, improved or shared» (Stewart, 1997: 74). Tacit knowledge could be shared by informal brainstorming meetings, using metaphors, stories and analogies, or with Stewart (1997: 73):»Tacit knowledge spreads when people meet and tell stories---».. This is done at Honda where they "set up brainstorming camps, informal meetings for detailed discussions to solve difficult problems in development project" (Nonaka & Takeuchi, 1995: 63). Keep in mind, however, that these meetings are focused upon tacit knowledge, not the brainstorming we usually are involved in, focusing upon explicit knowledge. The part of tacit knowledge which is linked to peoples experience carries with it, says Solow (1997: 4) :»a by-product, an automatic improvement in productivity». Solow (1997:20) also links the knowledge gained «somewhere on or close to the factory floor», i.e. tacit knowledge, to continuos innovation and «it leads to advances in customer satisfaction, in quality, durability, and reliability, and to continuing reductions in the cost of production».

Hidden knowledge is learned by socialization and could be shared in the business world, first of all by openly questioning our mental models (Senge, 1990), and second by using focus groups (Morgan, 1988; 1993). It is the willingness to question underlying assumptions, (Johnson, 1996)

, which in practical settings has to be focused. The use of focus groups gives access to uncodified knowledge, the language, mental models, the opinions, the meanings, the presuppositions, the world view of the participants. Focus groups also give the opportunity to make synergy of the individuals way of thinking as part of a collective.

Relationship knowledge is learned by interaction, and could be shared by systematic work in teams complementary composed. An example of developing relationship knowledge is Japanese firms bringing their supplier partners along with them when visiting European customers (Nonaka & Takeuchi, 1995). Both the firm and the supplier develop and strengthen relationships by this way, in addition to developing and strengthening relationship with the customers. In these contexts hidden knowledge also could be made explicit.

Based on the previous discussion we propose a scheme for information- and knowledge- management

Fig. 3 Information-and knowledge- management

Types of knowledge	Learning by	What is learned	How to share it	Media
Systemic knowledge	Studying patterns	Know why, i.e. new ways of thinking about "facts"	Computer simulation, scenario-planning etc.	Systemic tools
Explicit knowledge	Listening/ reading	Know what	Communication	Books, lectures electronic-media etc.
Tacit knowledge	Using/ doing/ experimenting	Know how	Stories, examples, metaphors, analogies, apprenticeship	Practical experience, apprenticeship relationship
Hidden knowledge	Socialization	Knowing how we know	Focus groups aimed at dialouge	Questioning underlying assumptions and mental models
Relationship knowledge	Interacting	Know who	Partnership and teamwork	Social settings

In the West we are good at creating and using knowledge which is easily communicated as information. In Japan according to Nonaka and Takeuchi (1995), they emphasize tacit knowledge for the innovation process. If it is possible to make knowledge which is difficult to communicate to others (tacit-, hidden-, systemic knowledge) explicable, then we could speed up learning-, transfer-, and innovation- processes in organizations.

In order to create knowledge for innovation we have to organize the process to make the knowledge which is difficult to communicate, understood by the people involved. This could be looked upon as a system integration and networking model, denoted by Rothwell (1995: 265-282) as the fifth generation innovation models. To make this happen we have to make tacit knowledge, hidden knowledge and systemic knowledge explicable in some way, in order to share it with other people.

ORGANIZATIONAL INNOVATION

Businesses are increasingly organized around processes, integration of people, knowledge integration, quality and service (Juran, 1989). These organizing features make traditional methods of organizing and managing increasingly ineffective (Johnson & Kaplan, 1987, Harrington, 1991, Hamel & Prahalad, 1994).

There seem to be a shift from functional organizing and functional management, to process-organizing and process-management (Hammer & Champy, 1993). The task of functional management is completed in different departments, while the task of process management is handed out in process-teams with a "hands-on" approach to the whole process (Lewis, 1995). Process organizing and process management as a new paradigm must be treated as a strategic corporate priority in the same way as Diamancescu (1992: 8) emphasizes cross-function-management. Both Total Quality Management (TQM), process innovation and Business Process Reengineering (BPR) are promising perspectives or mental models for this shift (Harrington, 1991).

Traditional ways of competing have reached a level of parity in which businesses can no longer easily distinguish themselves solely on the basis of technology, product, or price (Jacobson, 1992). The ability of an organization to conceptualize and manage change, to compete from the inside and out by increasing the learning capacity of its knowledge-workers, has become a competitive advantage in itself (Nonaka & Takeuchi, 1995). For organizations, the rise to primacy of knowledge workers creates both extraordinary opportunities and challenges, especially in the management of people (Drucker, 1993). The ideas and knowledge needed to create new products and services or to add value to old ones reside in the minds of individuals (Seagal & Horne, 1997). The role of the manager in the knowledge-based economy will be to manage the environment or context in which work is done, rather than controlling the workers themselves (Stewart, 1997, Thurow, 1996, Sveiby, 1997). The manager will serve as a coach and facilitator, a boundary-buster and head cheerleader. His or her role will be to eliminate the barriers that keep individuals from performing at their best. Success in the new economy requires a new form of vision-based leadership (Davenport, 1993: 117-137). Leaders must be involved in defining the mission and vision of the organization and developing and implementing plans to achieve the desired results (Sveiby, 1997).

The winning companies of the decade ahead will be those providing their people with the best weapons with which to compete, i.e. knowledge and service (Quinn, 1992, Quinn et. al., 1996). For most international competitors, the challenge is no longer simply quality. Quality has become a given. You cannot compete globally without it (Juran, 1989, Garbor, 1991). The challenge of the 21 st. century is productivity for the service and knowledge workers (Drucker, 1993), strategic flexibility and innovation. There is a growing awareness that productivity, quality and, hence competitive advantage are directly linked to the ability of organizations to learn and innovate, because the one sure source of lasting competitive advantage is knowledge (Yasuda, 1991, Solow, 1997, Thurow, 1997, Stewart, 1997, Sveiby, 1997).

The conventional Western approach to acquiring knowledge is through identifying hard, quantifiable data and universal procedures (Nonaka & Takeuchi, 1995). Western companies generally prefer cookbook solutions to problems of increased efficiency, lower costs, and improved return on investment (Juran, 1964, 1989).

By contrast, a handful of companies of the leading edge are beginning to unearth a more promising solution by trapping into the tacit, often subjective experiences, insights, and intuitions of individuals; especially those individuals who are high achievers (Peters, 1987, Peters & Waterman, 1982). A seven-year study of "knowledge workers" at Bell Labs, for example found that identifying the work strategies of an organizations top performers and making them available to other employees, productivity gain doubled.

People can become more effective by understanding the importance of the processes in which they are involved (Hammer & Champy, 1993; Hammer, 1996). To succeed in the new economy, these activities and processes must be designed and managed differently or with Johnson and Kaplan (1987: 229): "Process control must be accomplished at the level of the organization where the process occurs".

Rather than a "requisite variety" of function, what is needed is a "requisite variety" of continuos improvement and continuos innovation. More specifically "Every organization of today has to build into its very structure the management of change" (Drucker, 1993: 53).

Conclusion

Practical implications

Fig. 4 summarizes the practical part of this chapter

Fig 4 Information and knowledge management aimed at organizational- learning and- innovation

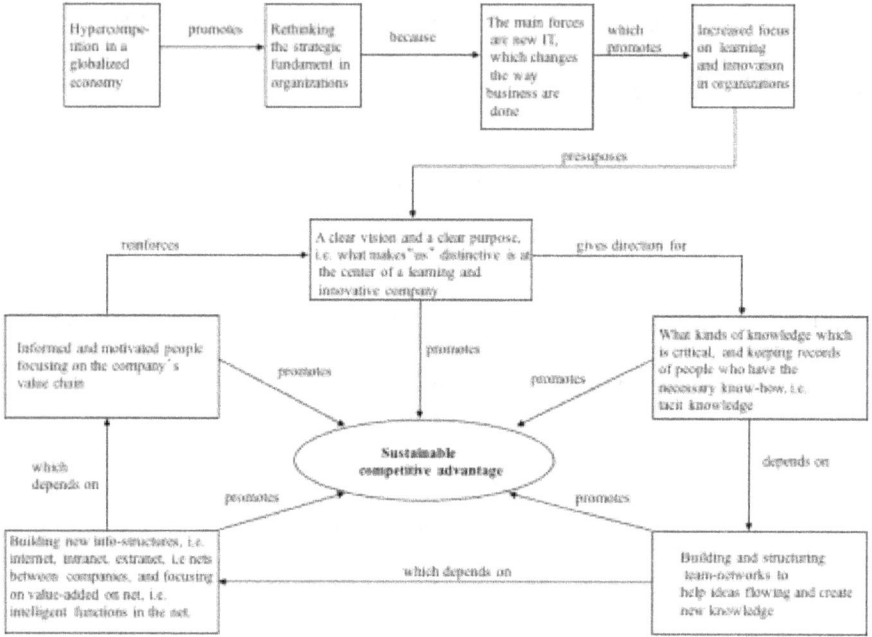

Theoretical implications

To understand what type of knowledge is essential in achieving e.g. innovative success, reflection on the company's normative basis is critical. The importance of the normative basis for the innovation process has also been denoted as "the encultural model of skill transmission" (Pinch, Collins & Carbone, 1996:164). This model has been contrasted to the transfer of knowledge as bits of information, or the linear model, i.e. R&D, inventions, innovations and transmission, also named the algorithmic model. The enculturational model has had a strong impact on innovation research (see Von Hippel & Tyre, 1995; Von Hippel, 1994; Nonaka & Tacheuchi, 1995). Lundval (1992:8) says: "Almost all innovations reflect already existing knowledge, combined in new ways".

Innovation is a major element in economic growth, and secure an improved competitive position for the companies (Solow, 1997). Innovation research is a fundamental study of change processes, knowledge development and knowledge integration, for the purpose of generating new combinations.

While the algorithmic or linear model focuses on explicit knowledge, the encultural or circular model (also denoted as the co-operation model, the interactive model and the cyclical model) emphasizes a system of relations between the following entities: R & D activities, structural links, tacit knowledge, interactive learning, the cultural context, social processes, national and regional innovation systems and customer and supplier relations (see Lundvall, 1992; Campagni, 1991:8). It is the emphasis on a variety of knowledge types, and the links between them which is regarded as the most valuable resource in the encultural model, and learning is regarded as the most important process. Another dominant feature pertaining to the encultural innovation model is the store set by collaboration, as opposed to the emphasis on competition (see Lundvall and Johnson, 1994:26; You and Wilkinson, 1994: 265).

The encultural innovation model observes the connection between organizational, technological, and environmental factors (see OECD, 1992; Smith, 1994; Klein and Rosenberg, 1986; Dosi, 1988; Malerba, 1992, European Commission, 1995). The model presupposes that innovation processes vary from company to company, and that there is a pattern of interactive processes which generates innovation activity in the companies.

The encultural model is based on theoretical assumptions for a more evolutionary economic theory (see Jacobsen 1992; Metcalfe, 1995:25-46) and knowledge derived from new economic growth theories (see Scott, 1989). In the encultural model R & D activities are not seen as the primary process generating innovations, but rather as part of a bigger system of relations among various elements: market contact, design, financial opportunities, the possibilities of linking the company to external knowledge systems, the use of information and communication technology, management skills, company culture, network activities and the regional and national innovation system (see Smith, 1994: 7-8; Klein and Rosenberg, 1986).

The research policy implications of the encultural model will be that the emphasis on research must turn more toward relations between elements generating innovation systems at various system levels, in order to disclose patterns hindering/promoting innovation in social systems. To achieve this goal several methods must be applied in the same research project or at least research program, e.g. statistical investigations, hypothesis testing, longitudinal studies, comparative studies and more angles of incidence based on action research. By using an interdisciplinary approach simultaneously, we may find ourselves in a position to disclose the system of relations between elements constituting a pattern which hinders/promotes innovation.

Based upon the arguments in this chapter we propose aspects of a theory of organizational innovation based on information-and knowledge management in fig. 5.

Fig. 5 Innovation theory based on information-and knowledge-management

ASSUMPTIONS
* Knowledge development, knowledge integration and knowledge application is the principal productive resource of the organization.
* The tacitness of a skill is a matter of degree.
* Organizations are systems integrating knowledge by transforming input into output, for the purpose of generating values for the customers/users

PROPOSITIONS

1. **Vision**
   A. A clear vision and a clear purpose indicates the direction for specific information search behaviour.

2. **Knowledge development**
   A. Single individuals' understanding of basic technology and the existing processes within the organization, determines the receptiveness for specific information, and indicates the direction for focused search activities and knowledge development.

3. **Knowledge integration**
   A. Knowledge is integrated most efficiently in team-based organizations, or virtual team-networks, focusing on the simultaneous existence of:
      a) What the organization is designed to do
      b) Core activities
      c) Core competence
      d) Explicit performance criteria
   B. Routines for effective structural connections(connectedness) enhance the innovation potential.
   C. The use of information technology to integrate knowledge increase the degree of innovation, but presupposes that information, communication and organizational learning systems take knowledge which is not easily communicate into consideration.

4. **Knowledge application**
   A. Organizational routines promote practical application of knowledge, and raises the organization's innovation level.
   B. Organizational routines based on master-apprentice organizing is conducive to the transformation of tacit knowledge and increases incremental innovations

IMPLICATIONS FOR ORGANIZATIONAL INNOVATION

A. A high degree of innovation presupposes relationships in teams based on trust and a basic helping attitude, in addition to common mental models and a performance culture in the entire organization.

B. A high degree of innovation presupposes internal and external structural connections (connectedness)

C. A high degree of innovation presupposes organizational learning systems which develop, integrate and use knowledge in the practical context

References

Ackoff, R.L.(1981). Creating the Corporate Future, John Wiley & Son, New York.

Ackoff, R.L.(1984). A Guide to Controlling your Corporate Future, John Wiley & Son, New York.

Archibugi, D. & Michie, J (1995). Technology and Innovation: An Introduction. Cambridge Journal of Economics, 19, 1-4.

Barney, J.B. (1991). Firm resources and sustained competitive advantage, Journal of Management, 17, 1: 99-120.

Beer, M., Eisenstat, A. & Spector, B. (1990). The critical path to corporate renewal, Harvard Business School Press, Boston.

Black, J.A. & Boal, K.B. (1994). Strategic resources: traits, configurations and paths to sustainable competitive advantage, Strategic Management Journal, 15 (summer special issue),: 131-148.

Bonoma, T.V. (1985). Case research in marketing: Opportunities, problems, and a process, Journal of Marketing Research, 22: 199-208.

Brynjolfsson, E. (1994). Technologys true payoff, Informationweek, 10 ocktober: 34-36.

Brynjolfsson, E. & Hitt, L. (1996). Paradox Lost? Firmlevel evidence on the returns to information system spending, Management Science, 42,4: 541-558.

Bunge, M. (1983). Exploring the World. Dordrecht: Reidel.

Camagni, R. (ed.), 1991, Innovation networks: spatial perspective,

Belhaven Press, London.

Collis, D.C. & Montgomery, C.A. (1995). Competing on resources: Strategy in the 1990´s, Harvard Business Review, 73 (July-August), : 118-128.

Czarniawska-Joerges, B. (1992). Exploring Complex Organizations, Sage, Newbury Park, CA.

DÁveni, R. (1994). Hypercompetition: Managing the dynamics of strategic maneuvering, The Free Press, New York.

Davenport, T.H. (1993). Process Innovation: Reengineering Work Through Information Technology, Harvard Business School Press, Boston, Massachusets.

David, P. & D. Foray (1995). Accessing and expanding the science and technology-base, STI-Review.

Diamancescu, D. (1992). The Seamless Enterprise: Managing Cross Functional Management Work", Harper Row, New York.

Dosi, G., 1988, Sources, procedures and microeconomic effect of innovation, Journal of Economic Litterature, 36, pp. 1126-71.

Drucker, P.F.(1993). Post-capitalist Society, Butterworth Heineman,

New York.

Eliason, G. (1996). Spillovers, integrated production and the theory of the firm, Journal of Evolutionary Economics, 6, 2: 125-140.

European Commission (1995). Green chapter on innovation, Brussel.

Evans, P.B. & Wurster, T.S. (1997). Strategy and the new economics of information, Harvard Business Review, sept-oct.: 71-84.

Fransman, M. (1990). The Market and Beyond, Co-operation and Competition in information Technology in the Japanese System, Cambridge University Press, Cambridge.

Freeman, C. (1995). The National System of Innovation in historical Perspective, Cambridge Journal of Economics, 19: 5-24.

Fruin, W.M. (1997). Knowledge Works: Managing intellectual capital at Toshiba, Oxford University Press Oxford.

Garbor, A.(1991). "The Man Who Discovered Quality", Random House, New York.

Grant, R.M. (1996). Prospering in dynamically competitive environments: Organizational capability as knowledge integration, Organizational Science, 7, 4: 375-387.

Hammer, M. (1996). Beyond Reengineering, Harper Collins, New York.

Hammer, M and Champy, J. (1993). Reengineering the Corporation, Harper Business, New York.

Hamel, G. & Prahalad, L.K. (1994). "Competing for the Future", Harvard Business School Press, Boston, Massachusetts.

Harrington, H.J. (1991). "Business Process Improvement", McGraw-Hill, New York.

Hart, S.L. (1995). "A Natural.Resource-Based View of the Firm". Academy of Management Review, Vol.20, No.4, 986-1014.

Heimer, C.A. (1992). Doing your job and helping your friends: Universalistic norms about obligations to particular others in networks. In Nohria, N. & Eccles, R.G. (eds.). Networks and organizations-Structure, form and actions, Harvard Business School Press, Boston, Mass. pp.: 143-164.

Howells, J. (1996). Tacit knowledge, innovation and technology transfer, Technology Analysis & Strategic Management, 8, 2: 91-105.

Iansiti, M. (1993). Real-World R&D: Jumping the Product Generation Gap, Harvard Business Review, May-June: 138-147.

Innis, R.E. (1994). Consciousness and the play of sign, Indiana University Press, Bloomington, Indianapolis.

Itami, H. & Roehl, T.W. (1987). "Mobilising invisible assets", Harvard University Press, Cambridge, MA.

Jacobsen, R., 1992, The austian school of strategy, Academy of Management Review, 17, 4, pp. 782-807.

Johannessen, J-A. (1996) Systemics applied to the study of organizational fields: Developing a systemic research strategy, Kybernetes, 25, 1: 33-50.

Johannessen, J-A. (1997). Aspects of causal processes, Kybernetes, 26, 1: 30-52.

Johannessen, J-A. (1998). Organisations as social systems: in search for a systemic theory of organisational innovation processes, Kybernetes, 27, 1-3

Johnson, H.T. & R.S. Kaplan (1987). Relevance Lost: The Rise and Fall of Management Accounting", Harvard Business School Press, Boston.

Juran, J.M. (1964). "Managerial Breakthrough", Mc Graw-Hill, New

York.

Juran, J.M. (1989). Juran on Leadership for Quality", The Free Press, New York.

Kanter, R. M. (1983). "The Change Masters", Unwin Hyman, London.

Kanter, R.M. (1986). "Creating the Creative Environment", Management Review, 75: 11-12.

Kanter, R.M., Stein, B.A. and Jock, T.D.(1992). "The Challenge of organizational Change: How Companies Experience it and Leaders Guide it", Free Press, NewYork.

Klein, S. and Rosenberg, N., 1986, An overview of innovation, in R.Landan and N. Rosenberg (ed.). The positive sum strategy, National Academy Press, Washington.

Knorr-Cetina, K.D. (1981). The Manufacture of knowledge: An Essay on the constructivist and contextual nature of science, Pergamon Press, Oxford.

Kuznets, S. (1966). Modern economic growth: Rate, structure, spread, Yale University Press, New Haven.

Laestadius, S. (1996). Competence requirements in low-tech firms, Journal of Vocational Training (Forthcomming).

Landabaso, M. (1995). The promotion of innovation in Regional Community Policy: Lessons and proposals for a regional innovation strategy, Chapter presented "International Workshop on Regional Science and Technology Policy Research, Himeji, Japan, 13-16 feb.

Leonard-Barton, D.L. (1995). Wellsprings of Knowledge: Building and Sustaining the Sources of Innovation, Harvard Business School Press, Boston, MASS.

Lewis, J.D. (1995). "The Connected Corporation", The Free Press, New York.

Luhmann, N. (1986). The autopoiesis of social systems. In F. Geyer and J. van der Zouwen (eds.). Sociocybernetic Paradoxes. Sage. Beverly Hills, CA. pp. 172-192.

Luhmann, N. (1992). Ecological Communication. Polity Press. Cambridge.

Lundvall, B.Å. (ed.)., 1992, National systems of innovation, Pinter, London.

Lundvall, B-Å. (1995). Inaugural Lecture, Department of Business Studies, Aalborg University, Nov. 10.

Lundvall, B.Å. and Johnson, B.,1994, The learning economy, Journal of industry studies, 1, 2 pp. 23-42.

Mahoney, J.T. and Pandian, J. R (1992). "The resource-based view within the conversation of strategic managemnt". Strategic Management Journal, Vol. 13, 363-380.

Malerba, F., 1992, The organization of the innovative process, in N. Rosenberg; R. Landan and D. Mowery (eds.), pp. 247-280, Technology and the wealth of nations, , Stanford University Press, Stanford.

Maturana, H.R. & Varela, F.J. 1987 The tree of Knowledge, New Science Library, London.

McGrath, R.G; MacMillan, I.C & Venkataraman, S. (1995). "Defining and developing competence: A strategic process paradigm". Strategic Management Journal, Vol. 16, 251- 275.

Metcalfe, J.S., 1995, Technology systems and technology policy in an evolutionary framework, Cambridge Journal of Economics, 19 pp. 25-46.

Mintzberg, H. (1978). Patterns in strategy formation, Management

Science, 24, 9: 934-948.

Mintzberg, H. (1979). The structuring of organizations, Prentice Hall, Englewood, Cliffs, N.J.

Mintzberg, H. (1983). Structures in Fives: Designing effective organizations, Prentice Hall, Englewood, Cliffs, N.J.

Mintzberg, H. 81987). Crafting strategy, Harvard Business Review, 64 July-August, : 66-75.

Mintzberg,H. (1989). Mintzberg on Management, The Free Press, New York.

Morgan, D.L. (1988). Focus Groups as Qualitative Research, Sage, New York.

Morgan, D.L.(ed.). (1993). Succesful Focus Groups, Sage, New York.

Nisbet, R.A. (1969). Social Change and History: Aspects of the Western Theory of Development, Oxford University Press, Oxford.

Nonaka, K. (1991). The Knowledge creating company, Harvard Business Review, Nov.-dec.

Nonaka, I. (1994). A dynamic theory of organizational knowledge creation, Organizational Science, 5, 1: 14-37.

Nonaka, I. & Takeuchi, H. (1995). The Knowledge Creating Company, Oxford University Press, Oxford

OECD, 1992, Technology and the economy: the key relationships, Paris, OECD.

Parker, G.M. (1994). "Cross-Functional Teams", Jossey Bass, New York.

Peters, T. (1987). "Thriving on Chaos", Alfred A. Knoph, New York.

Peters, T.J. & Waterman, R. (1982). "In Search of Excellence", Harper & Row, New York.

Pinch, T., H.M. Collins & L. Carbone (1996). Inside Knowledge: Second order measures of skill, The Sociological Review, 44, 2: 163-187.

Polanyi, M. (1958). Personal knowledge, Personal Knowledge, Routledge & Kegan Paul, London

Polanyi, M. (1962). "Knowledge and Being", Routledge, New York.

Polanyi, M. (1966). The tacit dimension, Routledge & kegan Paul, London.

Prahalad, C.K. & Hamel, G. (1994). Strategy as a field of study: Why search for a new paradigm, Strategic Management Journal, 15 (Summer special issue), : 5-16.

Prahalad, C.K. & Hamel, G. (1996). Competing in the new economy: Managing out of bounds, Strategic Management Journal, 15: 237-242.

Quinn, J.B. (1992). "Intelligent Enterprise", The Free Press, New York.

Quinn, J.B, P. Anderson & S. Finkelstein (1996). Leveraging intellect, Academy of Management Executives, 10, 3: 7-27.

Reed, R. & DeFillippi, R. (1990). "Causal ambiguity, barriers to imitation, and sustainable competitive advantage", Academy of Management Review, 15: 88-102.

Reich, R.B., 1991, The work of nations, Alfred A. Knop, New York.

Rothwell, R. (1995). The Changing Nature of the Innovation Process: Implications for SME´s. In D.P.O´Doherty (Ed.). pp. 265-282. Globalization Networking and Smal Firm Innovation, Graham N. Trotman, London.

Sadler, P. (1988). Managerial leadership in Post-industrial society, Gower Publishing Company, Aldershot, Hants.

Schaaf, D. (1995). "Keeping the Edge", Penguin Books, New York.

Scott, M.F., 1989, A new view of economic growth, Clarendon Press, Oxford.

Schutz, A. (1990). The Problem of Social Reality. Collected Chapters, Vol. 1, 2 og 3. Kluwer Academic Publishers, London.

Seagal, S. & Horne, D. (1997). Human Dynamics: A new framework for understanding people and realizing the potential in our organizations, Pergasus Communications, Cambridge,MA.

Senge, P.M. (1990). "The Fifth Dicipline. The Art and Practice of the Learning Organization", Doubleday/ Currency, New York.

Smith, K., 1994, New direction in research and technology policy: Identifying the key issues, STEP rapport, nr. 1, Oslo.

Solow, R.M. (1997). Learning from learning by doing: Lessons for economic growth, Stanford University Press, Stanford, California.

Stehr, N. (1994). Knowledge societies, Sage, London.

Stewart, T.A. (1997). Intellectual capital: The new wealth of organizations, Doubleday, London.

Sveiby, K.E. (1997). The new organizational wealth: managing & measuring knowledge- based assets, Berrett-Koehler, San Francisco.

Teece, D.J. (1986). Profiting from technological innovation: Implication for integration, collaboration, licensing and public policy. I D.J. Teece (red.) The competitive Challenge: Strategies for industrial innovation and Renewal, Ballinger, Cambridge, MA.

Teece, D.J. (1988). The nature and the structure of firms. I G. Dosi, C.Freeman, R.Nelson, G. Silverberg & L. Soete (red.). Technical Change and Economic Theory, Pinter, London.

Thurow, L.C. (1996). The future of capitalism, Nicolas Brealey publishing, London.

Toffler, A., 1990, Powershift: knowledge, wealth and violence at the Edge of the 21 st. Century, Bantam Books, New York.

Tusman, M. & D. Nadler (1986). Organizing for Innovation, California Management Review, vol. 28, 3: 74-92.

Vleck, D.J. & Davidson, J.P. (1992). "The Domino Effect", Irwin, Homewood, IL.

Von Hippel, E. (1994). Sticley information and the locus of problem solving: Implication for innovation, Management Science, 40: 429-439.

Von Hippel, E. & M. Tyre (1995). How learnings by doing is done: Process equipment, Research Policy, 24: 1-12.

Weick, K.E. (1979). "The Social Psychology of Organizing", Addison-Wesley Publishing Company, London.

Whipp, R., Rosenfeld, R. & Pettigre, A. (1987). Understanding strategic change processes: Some preliminary British findings. In Pettigrew, A. (Ed.). The management of strategic change, Blackwell, London, pp.:14-55.

Whipp, R & Pettigrew, A. (1993). Leading change and the management of competition. In Hendry, J., Johnson, G. & Newton, J. (eds.). Strategic thinking and the management of change, John Wiley, pp.: 199-228.

Winter, S. (1987). "Knowledge and Competence as Strategic Assets". In D. Teece (Ed.), The Competitive Challenge: 159-184. Cambridge, MA: Ballinger.

Womack, J. P., Jones, D.T. & Roos, D. (1990). The machine that changed the world, Rawson, New York.

Yasuda, Y. (1991). "40 Years-20 Million ideas", Productivity Press, Cambridge, MA.

You, J.L. and Wilkinson, F., 1994, Competition and co-operation: toward understanding industrial districs, Review of Political Economy, 6,3 pp. 259-278.

CHAPTER 2 High-tech value creation

Introduction

When turbulence, discontinuity, uncertainty and ambiguity in the business environment are taken into account, it becomes possible to perceive how new knowledge may develop in organisations. According to knowledge theory, intuitive ideas about how new knowledge will emerge are based on information (Pfeffer & Sutton, 2000). Knowledge of the relevant information is necessary in order to anticipate where new knowledge will emerge and be realised through innovation. For instance, throughout history we know that transformations have taken place at certain time intervals and that new knowledge has emerged. However, we do not know if and when transformation will happen again in the future, or what knowledge will be translated into new technology within a market. Fundamental technical changes often lead to new knowledge and sometimes this knowledge is so extensive that it can result in what is known as paradigm shifts (Kuhn, 2013). We also know that when paradigm shifts are extensive they may lead to institutional innovations (North, 1990), which we here will term innovative transformations of society.

We also know with a high degree of probability that some changes emerge and lead to what Schumpeter terms "business cycles" (Schumpeter, 1954). Other types of changes also emerge, which may lead to economic cycles, more seldom than Schumpeter's "business cycles", but more pervasive, which are termed "long waves" of 40–60 years by Kondratiev (see Hirooka, 2006) among others. Although there are questions and debate concerning such cyclical theories, we know with a great degree of certainty that small and large fundamental changes continuously take place. We are therefore concerned with discussing the development of new knowledge, because this is crucial to the development of innovation and economic growth in societies (Audretsch, 2006).

In order to apply new knowledge in a market, three elements must be present (Gratton, 2007; Schumpeter, 1954; Hirooka, 2006):

- Organisational and management skills
- An understanding of the new global market
- The ability to focus on that which is unique

The organisational requirements that will facilitate the development and application of new knowledge may be described in relation to the necessity of the simultaneous existence of co-operation and co-creation

(Gratton, 2007), but the degree of co-creation and co-operation can vary greatly. Managerial preconditions may be described in relation to two concepts, namely value creation and value destruction, which may be structured into five focus areas (see Thakor, 2000):

- An understanding of the purpose of value creation
- An understanding of the various value creation perspectives
- An understanding of an organisation's strategy and the development of strategies that support this strategy
- The ability to develop methods for measuring value creation
- The ability to develop rapid responses to market signals

The "new market" is relatively well known as a concept related to the global knowledge economy. However, what is less known is that it involves a new way of thinking in relation to value creation in the global market. Drucker (1995: 143) mentions four dimensions that we should reflect on in relation to the new market that is emerging:

- The structure of the global market
- Changes in trade in the global market
- The importance of financial capital in the global market

- The relationship between global markets and organisations in a local context

In order to apply and exploit the development of new knowledge in the new market, it is crucial that individual organisations develop creative energy fields (Gratton, 2007) because this will enable them to continuously develop innovations and thereby gain competitive advantages in the global knowledge economy (op. cit). Those organisations that do this will most probably become more involved in high-tech value creation, which will result in high labour productivity and relatively low labour costs, enabling them to compete outside the area where low-cost countries operate. What one can sense in relation to the contours of the new knowledge economy is a greater emphasis on global clusters of expertise at the expense of local industrial clusters. It is reasonable to assume that global clusters of expertise will function as the social mechanisms for high-tech value creation, because the knowledge required to produce, distribute and reintegrate high-tech value creation is found throughout the global knowledge economy. The question we will examine here is what is needed to develop high-tech value creation in organisations? We illustrate this introduction in Figure 1, which also shows how the chapter is structured.

Fig. 1 High-tech. value creation

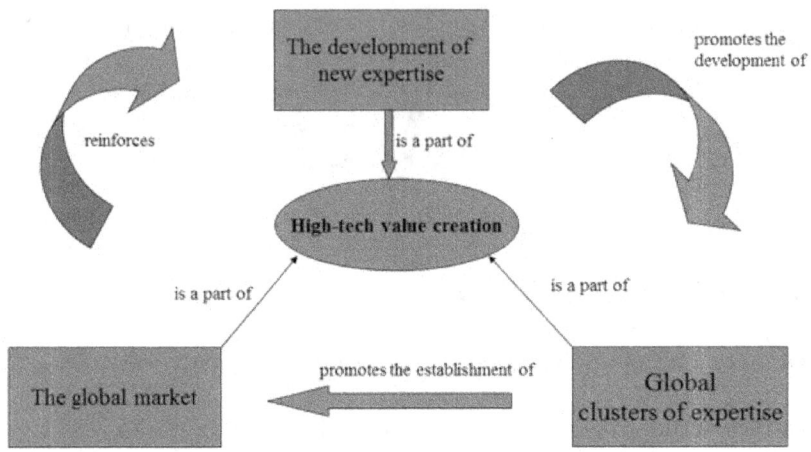

The development of new expertise

Without the hindsight of history, we cannot be certain about whether we are living in a period of fundamental changes, where new paradigms are emerging, or to what degree transformations are already taking place. An understanding of new knowledge may similarly be compared with the Owl of Minerva that only spreads its wings at the fall of dusk; in other words, a complete understanding of emerging knowledge is often only possible with hindsight. However, many signals suggest that we are living in an age where new ways of thinking are emerging. Drucker (1995: 75), as one example, notes that "our age is such a period of transformation".

We do not know with certainty what drives the transformation to which Drucker refers. Drucker (1995) and Thurow (2000), among others, point to the development of new knowledge, greater integration within and between social systems and the development of new technology as being important social mechanisms that contribute to this transformation. Knowledge, knowledge integration and new technology mutually reinforce each other and encourage the breakthrough of new ways of thinking about economic, political, social and cultural phenomena (Schumpeter, 1954; Drucker, 1999, Tsoukas & Shepherd, 2004).

We know that knowledge resources and customers are critical for most organisations in the global knowledge economy (Drucker, 1995; Collins, 1993). The knowledge that creates uniqueness in organisations is often specialised (Cooper, 1986). Increasingly, today, there are more specialists and more specialised professions such as gene research and bio-technological research, and there is also an increase in specialisation in increasingly smaller fields of knowledge. Yet, we have increasingly less knowledge about the totality, i.e. the larger patterns and relationships (Drucker, 1999; Sennett, 2007, 2008). Thus, an understanding of contexts, context expertise and insight into the development of patterns seems to be contrary to specialisation and expertise development. It seems that the more specialised knowledge developed, the less understanding we have of the context in which knowledge is developed.

It is in this situation that innovators and entrepreneurs can intervene with three measures (Drucker, 1995, 1999; Audretsch, 2006; Bicak, 2005). Firstly, they can apply their specialist knowledge or that of others to meet a demand. Secondly, they can use their understanding of patterns to place specialist knowledge in a broader context. Thirdly, they can transform existing organisations from the inside so that they can adapt to the new market, which they are also helping create. However, the new market is still at a premature stage, i.e. there is potentiality not actuality, and it is still waiting for entrepreneurs and innovators and their creative solutions.

Drucker (1995: 75) writes: "If history is any guide, this transformation will not be completed until 2010 or 2020." If we are in the midst of such a process of transformation, we cannot have any detailed knowledge on how this will unfold. However, we may be able to say a lot about the "bigger picture", because there will always be a lag between new knowledge and new technology. At a theoretical level, we know that there will be further tension between stability and change (Luhmann,

1996; Bateson, 1972: 272). We also know with a great degree of certainty that social networks will become increasingly more important (Strathdee, 2008), and that skills, talent and innovation will become increasingly important in the global knowledge economy (Jansen et al., 2007; Johannessen et al., 1999). We also know that environmental awareness and the social responsibility of organisations will become increasingly important (Werther & Chandler, 2005).

At a general level, we know a lot about how new knowledge will emerge, but as mentioned above, we know little of the details. What we do know is that the needs, wants, preferences and expectations at one level may indicate something about the specific developments that will emerge. However, taking needs, wants, preferences and expectations as a starting point will only reveal half the truth, because new knowledge also creates new needs, wants, preferences and expectations (Drucker, 1999). If, for instance, you had asked the man in the street in the 1960s about his need for a cell phone or laptop, his response would have given us little indication of the developments in the area of communication technology today. There was, of course, both telephony and computing in the 1970s, but these tools took radically different forms from what we know today. As evidenced in innovation research, it can often take 20–40 years before technological innovations make an impact (North, 1990;

Schumpeter, 1954; Roberts, 1991). It is also important to remember that many types of innovations do not to any large extent meet existing needs, but rather create new ones (Schumpeter, 1954; Sennett, 2007).

Based on what is described above, leaders should relate to two kinds of knowledge processes. Firstly, the knowledge that shows the needs, wants, preferences and expectations that relate to the functions of early warning systems used in organisations. Secondly, the knowledge developed in various public and private research foundations around the world. This knowledge can lead to new technology, which both creates needs and meets existing demand.

Knowledge is often divided into two main categories: explicit (codifiable) and tacit knowledge (Nonaka & Takeuchi, 1995). Explicit knowledge can be relatively easily formulated by using words, figures and symbols, it can be digitised (Nonaka & Takeuchi, 1995) and it can be relatively easily communicated to others by using ICT. This may be one of the reasons why explicit knowledge is often emphasised in collaboration projects compared with other kinds of knowledge that cannot be digitised. Tacit knowledge is rooted in action (practice) and is connected to specific contexts (Polanyi, 1962, 1966). It is difficult to communicate this type of knowledge to others in the form of information, because it is difficult to digitise. Tacit knowledge is often the most important strategic resource of organisations, because it is difficult for others to acquire and utilise it and because it is rooted in the specific problems that an organisation has to solve (Nonaka & Takeuchi, 1995). Tacit knowledge can thus be described as an important strategic capability of organisations (Grant, 2003: 211).

In addition to these two types of knowledge, two other types are also important: hidden knowledge (Kirzner, 1982; Grant, 2003) and implicit knowledge (Bicak, 2005). Hidden knowledge is that we do not know what we do not know and which many claim constitutes the basis for creativity and innovation (Kirzner, 1982: 273), or "the management of ignorance", which is "the key issue for companies as it is for society" (Grant, 2003: 222). Kirzner (1982) expresses explicitly that hidden knowledge provides opportunities for developing something that is creative and new, namely that "people do not know what it is that they do not know" (p. 273). Hidden knowledge, as it is described here, can be affected by ICT-based interaction.

Implicit knowledge is the knowledge an organisation possesses, but which is not utilised or put into productive practice, because knowledge boundaries prevent the integration of what an organisation knows.

Consequently, organisations are "dumber than they need to be", i.e. they do not exploit their potential (see Pfeffer & Sutton, 2000). Tacit, explicit, hidden and implicit knowledge can be developed through collective learning processes within an organisation, where, among other things, ICT-based interaction and knowledge development are essential. In addition, the transfer of experience and simple systematic organisational learning systems are also important. Innovation and the development of knowledge in organisations can be accomplished through a continuous dialogue between tacit, implicit, hidden and explicit knowledge (Polanyi, 1966; Wenger et al., 2002; Hedberg et al., 2002).

The new skills needed to compete in the global knowledge economy may be said to lie in the intersection between the four types of knowledge described above. The interaction and integration of knowledge takes place in what we have termed the "knowledge window" as shown in Figure 2. We assume here that new knowledge will emerge in what we have termed above as "global clusters of expertise", which we will examine in detail in the next section of the chapter.

Fig. 2 Knowledge integration

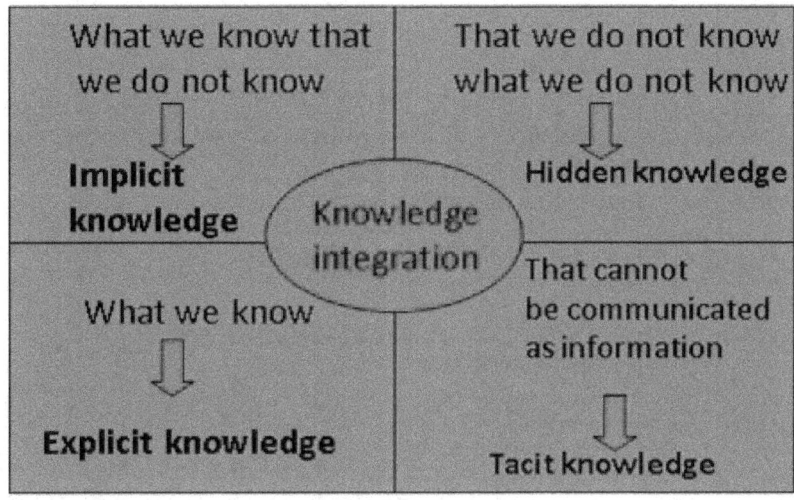

Global clusters of expertise

When needs and wants in a market are coupled with new technological knowledge, this often becomes the start of high-tech success stories (Rifkin, 1988). In addition, relationships, networks and co-creation are the central features of high-tech value creation (Kanter, 2006: 874). High-tech value creation also seems to attract complementary technological expertise and service companies (Wenger et al., 2002; Audretsch, 2006; Breschi & Malerba, 2007). After a period of time, local clusters develop and grow into separate social systems and these clusters grow through reputation, innovation and networking contacts. Examples of such local clusters are numerous, such as Silicon Valley, Route 128 (the Boston area), the Milan region and Paris, just to name a few.

We can recognise the contours of nations and regions that specialise in high-tech value creation within global clusters of expertise, such as Finland, India, China, Vietnam and South Korea. These global clusters are connected to, but independent of, local industrial clusters. Examples of emerging global clusters of expertise are the contracts and projects distributed globally online on different network platforms such as Elance.com. In this network, knowledge workers operate in the fields of marketing, IT, creative work and so on.

The expertise and technology that formed the basis for local industrial clusters often become after a period of time a part of the social systems that develop in global clusters of expertise. The expertise and technology in local industrial clusters are a necessary precondition for the development of global clusters of expertise, but this is not a sufficient condition for their survival. Metaphorically, the technology and expertise in local industrial clusters may be said to be the midwife of the expertise that is developed in and around global clusters of expertise. In other words, the technology that was developed in local clusters often triggers the skills and expertise used in global clusters. The new expertise creates in turn new technologies that promote economic growth within and outside global clusters.

There are a number of differences between local industrial clusters and global clusters. Firstly, local clusters are located geographically, while global clusters are virtually organised into a system of various networks: technological, psychological, cultural and social. Secondly, local clusters are physically visible and provide a tangible return, while global clusters are "invisible" and their value is not recorded in separate audit reports and the like. Thirdly, local clusters are often governed by hierarchical principles, while global clusters are governed by "a flocking principle", i.e. in a flock of birds, a school of herring and so on, where the behaviour of the group is guided by fundamental principles and procedures rather than a leader.

It may be argued that high-tech value creation requires more active public and private support than is necessary in the so-called projects of traditional entrepreneurs, because the complexity and resource requirements are much greater in the former. It is not sufficient to let the processes of creative destruction alone decide the development of high-tech value creation in global clusters. Consequently, clear and unambiguous public policies for participation in global clusters should be developed.

The processes of creative destruction should also be controlled through public policies concerning what kind of development is desirable, especially in cases when governments invest a large amount of resources over a period of time into infrastructure, info-structure, expertise building and various types of capital in global clusters. Through global clusters of expertise, the locomotive principle will come into effect and this will reinforce itself through the development of new activities, expertise and technology. Global clusters of expertise will consequently be both pulled and pushed forward by public policies (Cooper, 1986).

We illustrate the difference between local industrial clusters and global clusters of expertise in Figure 3. Global clusters of expertise may also be understood in relation to "coordination logic" as shown in Figure 6, where information and communication are the functional areas of the global expertise network. Information and communication operate at global and virtual levels, creating ideas and innovations for local industrial clusters.

Fig. 3 Local industrial clusters and global clusters of expertice

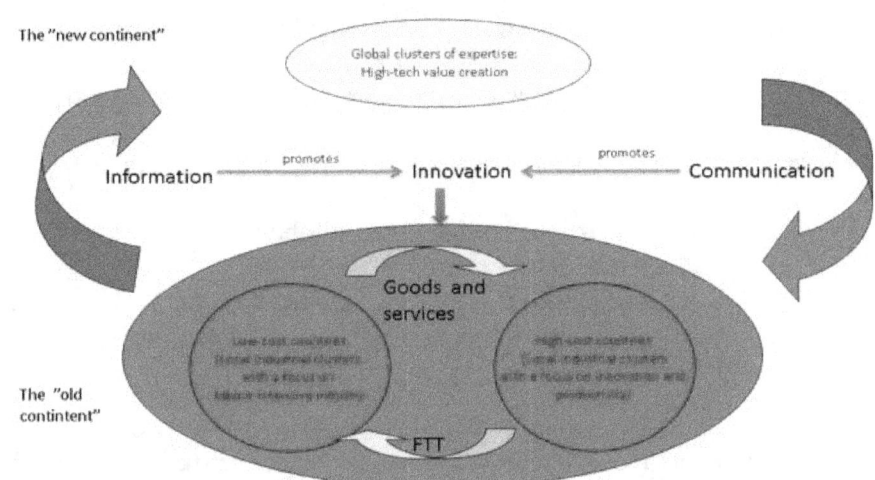

FTT= Finance-technology, transport-technology, telecommunications-technology

Established enterprises, entrepreneurs and innovators can offer their expertise[2], talent[3], ideas and burning desire either when starting up their own enterprises or when changing existing businesses, which is a necessary precondition for developing high-tech value creation. However, unless national policies are implemented to stimulate

---

[2] "Expertise" here may be divided into three components: knowledge, skills and attitudes.

[3] "Talent" here may be divided into five components: willpower, initiative, quality, creativity and commitment.

development and participation in global clusters of expertise, then expertise and talent may not be sufficient when establishing regional or national modules in global clusters. Expertise and talent may be a necessary precondition, but the appropriate national policies are a sufficient condition if regions or nations are to participate in global clusters of expertise. Global clusters of expertise thus encourage the development of various types of networks, alliances and federations, i.e. loosely structured organisations working together to integrate knowledge (Handy, 1992).

Co-operation and co-creation seem to be characteristic of thinking in global clusters of expertise. In Kanter's (2006: 860) international cultural studies, the following characteristics of effective[4] organisations emerged:

- "Departments collaborate
- Conflicts are viewed as creative
- People can do anything not explicitly prohibited
- Decisions are made by the people with the most knowledge."

In relation to high-tech value creation the following conclusions may

---

[4] Effectiveness in Kanter's studies was subjectively evaluated by respondents.

be drawn from Kanter's cultural studies. First, the global expertise network has a front-line focus and organisations must be designed around a specific purpose. Kanter (2006: 860) terms this "communities of purpose". This means that organisations evolve to become part of a larger integrated whole in global clusters. However, organisations are independent and stand alone in global knowledge networks. They are also part of a larger complex social system with a common purpose within limited areas. Metaphorically, the factory walls are blown apart and production is globally distributed in relation to the logic of costs, quality, expertise, talent and innovation, which is summarised in Figure 6 by using the term "distribution logic". In this way, some organisations are included in the global expertise network, while others are excluded and risk becoming a global economic backwater.

With a common understanding of the purpose of global clusters of expertise, i.e. networks, alliances or federations, it becomes easier to respond quickly to the emerging elements of knowledge in one location in global clusters in order to transform this into new technology and receive a payback in another location in the network. This type of knowledge integration promotes the development of new technology and high-tech value creation, because loosely coupled global clusters will be able to react quickly and use skills and talents toward a common purpose and thereby create innovations (Drucker, 1999; Sennett, 2007).

Co-operation and co-creation are two different things (Uzzi, 1997, Adler & Kwon, 2002), although co-operation in some cases can lead to co-creation. However, co-operation is possible without co-creation, and co-creation is possible without a great deal of co-operation (op. cit). On the other hand, co-operation and co-creation can lead to personal triumphs and organisational productivity (Gratton, 2007). Co-creation is defined here as "activities that focus productive practices related to an organization's purpose", whereas co-operation is defined as "all the other activities in an organization that players perform together, but which are not directly linked to productive practices related to an organization's purpose". However, different types of expertise must exist in an organisation to allow various degrees of co-operation and co-creation, as illustrated in Figure 4.

A low level of co-operation and co-creation will necessitate that an organisation possesses specific expertise in one area, which can promote productivity. When there is a low level of co-operation but a high level of co-creation, a high level of integration of expertise will be required in the organisation, because co-creation by itself does not allow the necessary integration between individuals and across teams. This expertise will promote continuous improvements in the organisation. Similarly, a high level of co-operation but a low level of co-creation will require the existence of creative expertise in the organisation. This expertise will be able to promote the development of ideas in the organisation. When there is a high level of both co-operation and co-creation, then the requirements are fulfilled to promote a high level of innovation, because the creation of new innovations is promoted under such conditions (see Wenger et al., 2002). To avoid "chaos", however, organisations in global clusters of expertise must focus on the field of innovation, where the four types of knowledge are integrated (Lave & Wenger, 1991).

Organisations that participate in global clusters of expertise should ensure that these different types of expertise exist under the various degrees of co-operation and co-creation. The above description is illustrated in Figure 4.

Figure 4. Typology of expertise under various conditions in relation to promoting innovation

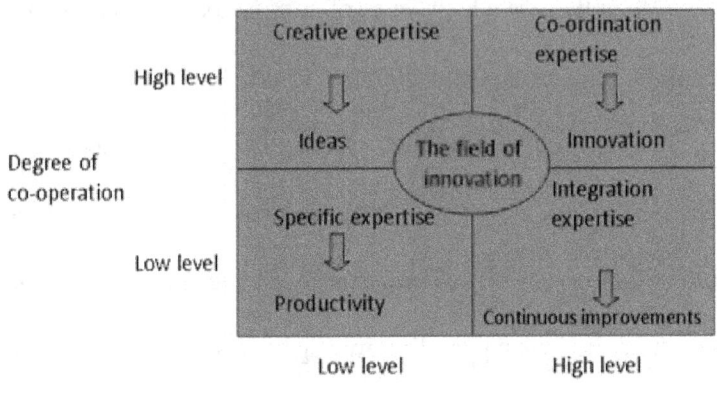

In order to promote co-operation, it is important that the physical and psychological distances between teams and project members are reduced (Gratton, 2002). Furthermore, it is essential that conflicts, problems and disagreements are handled in a satisfactory manner, i.e., organisations should develop conflict management skills (op. cit). Co-operation also requires that players develop positive relationships based on mutual support (Egan, 1977).

The first condition for promoting co-creation is that players focus on productive practices, or the purpose of what they have set out to do, because co-creation is linked to results, which is not necessarily the case with co-operation (see Flynn et al., 2001). The second condition for promoting co-creation is the synchronisation of work so that both the parts and the whole are taken care of because the complexity of most high-tech projects is very high (Vinton, 1992). The third condition for promoting co-creation is the introduction of rhythm to the work process because knowledge workers need to combine autonomy with an understanding of results (see Waller et al., 2001).

The global market

Changes in the global market occur at a rapid pace owing to new skills and technology and economic and institutional innovations (North, 1990; Drucker, 1999; Sennett, 2007). One of the emerging institutional innovations has been described above, namely global clusters of expertise. In particular, the pace of change is increasing because there is a growing link between new technology and new expertise, represented in Figure 4 as the field of innovation.

It seems that we must develop a new "sense of direction" when our mental maps no longer match the terrain, because our fundamental experiences have collapsed as the pace of change has increased so rapidly. Our "sense of direction" is here understood as our understanding of new trends. With this understanding, we can move around without a "map" in a new environment, because we have developed a sense of what is happening, what will happen in the future as well as how and why, and what possible effects it can have on the organisation and other social systems.

This understanding may be developed in many ways; for instance, through what is often termed "foresight" (Tsoukas & Shepherd, 2004), which implies gaining an understanding of the new global market emerging. In this context, individuals with "foresight" have been described as "those that can accurately predict forthcoming changes and effectively implement a series of steps/actions to exploit them before their competitors" (Tsoukas & Shepherd, 2004: xiii).

Nevertheless, if the terrain changes so quickly that our maps become outdated, we cannot wait until we have up-to-date information before making a decision, because the organisation may lose its position in the market relatively quickly. Consequently, if the market changes faster than our mental models of how the market behaves, we must attempt to conceptualise rather than specify concretely what we think is about to happen.

Conceptualisation is an abstraction process whereby you select one element while discarding another. The essence is to focus on what you have selected, making a conceptual generalisation. Normann (2004: 296) writes the following about the importance of this process: "Unless we are able to creatively conceptualize a territory which a priori lends itself to any kind of interpretation or any intellectual viewpoint, we will be lost … And so action orientation and conceptual thinking are two sides of the same coin".

Let us illustrate this conceptual generalisation process through the concept of creative energy fields, which we have associated with Gratton's (2007) term "hot spot". Firstly, there is a difference between creative energy fields and that which manifests itself from creative energy fields. Secondly, creative energy fields exist at various levels (micro, meso, macro). Thirdly, different social mechanisms may trigger these creative energy fields at various levels. Fourthly, there are countless creative energy fields at various levels. Fifthly, creative energy fields are most likely connected through global clusters of expertise at all levels, and possibly between levels. The point of illustrating a conceptualisation process with a focus on creative energy fields at various levels is, among other things, to show that the new global market is ubiquitous and that it consists of various systems of creative energy fields at the micro, meso and macro levels.

The new market is concrete and virtual at the same time. Therefore, organisations must also free themselves from physical, mental and geographical boundaries. At the policy level, the free flow of goods, labour and services drives market development. The virtual connections at the macro level consist of what might be termed the production, distribution and consumption of symbols; this consists of information and knowledge organisations. While factories in the industrial society were linked to the land on which they were built, the knowledge industry is mainly virtual, i.e. distributed globally according to the logic of costs, quality, expertise, talent and innovation (see Figure 6).

When organisations flow out into the global space in this way, a vacuum occurs locally, as they are "more vulnerable to invaders attacking their previous local dominance" (Normann, 2004: 297). While organisations before had a territory, to use a biological analogy, in which they had their niche which encompassed their habitat, in the new market a different situation has occurred. The habitat becomes both the territory and the niche through the fact that organisations become both global and virtual, where absolutely all the boundaries are transient.

When organisations become mainly virtual, driven by the logic of the five elements of costs, quality, expertise, talent and innovation, it does not mean that they are less real or that they are moving around in the global space without an anchor. Organisations are visible locally, but they also operate where they cannot be seen physically. They are fragmented in real and virtual modules like Lego bricks. These Lego bricks/modules are governed by an overall design and reintegrated locally. Some of these Lego modules are distributed where costs are low when this is preferable, while other modules are distributed where quality is highest. Other modules are distributed where skills such as design expertise are the highest, while other modules are distributed where talent and innovation potential is the highest. Individual modules can thus be concerned with one product or several products or services. Only rarely will a local geographic area meet the requirements of the five elements described above. That is why we say that the habitat has become both territory and niche.

The new market is not visible in the traditional sense and it cannot be defined as a system of demand and supply, which was the case in the industrial society. The reason is that the customers' needs, wants, preferences and expectations are just as important as demand. These four elements drive the creative energy fields in the new market and, to a lesser extent, real demand. It is not possible to say either that there is supply-driven demand, because supply is a result of creative energy fields and not vice versa. It is the balance between creative chaos/creative energy fields and the needs, wants, preferences and expectations among potential and existing customers that drives the new market forward (Schumpeter, 1954; Kirzner, 1982; Normann, 2004; Lucia, 2004). In this way, demand is de-emphasised as a social mechanism for organisations and the early warning systems that can identify the needs, wants, preferences and expectations of potential future customers are given more emphasis.

One of the consequences for players in creative energy fields is that they must learn to live with creative chaos where everything is fluid. In turn, players have to relate to a situation where the boundary between competition and co-operation is also fluid. Figure 5 shows a visual representation of the above description.

Figure 5. High-tech value creation: a conceptual schema

Dimensions / Distinctions (Level)	Social mechanisms	Global clusters of expertise
Macro	**Policies at national and regional levels:** Free flow of goods, services and labour	**Virtual connections** Production, distribution and consumption of symbols that create distinctions
Meso	**Organizational capabilities** Driven forward by a logic of costs, quality, expertise, talent and innovation	**Organizational alliances of various kinds** Logic of distribution based on modules (Lego - organization)
Micro	**Players in creative energy fields** Players must learn to live with creative chaos	**The players relationships and networks** Fluid boundaries between competition and co-operation

In order to further concretise and exemplify parts of this development, we will refer to the fishing industry. While the fisherman, the fish and the fishing industry were in the past geographically closely linked, namely the industry was located close to the raw materials and the fisherman was, as a rule, located close to the fish resources, now the situation is such that:

1. In the case of global aquaculture, traditional fishermen no longer have a function.

2. In the case of industrial trawlers, local fishing areas are no longer involved, because trawlers catch the fish, freeze them on board

and transport them, for example, to places such as China, for processing. The finished products are then transported back to the old fishing village and the market in general. Obviously, this development results in a change in character for many local communities. The fisherman, or at least the fisherman's children if they remain in the fishing village, will become participants in the global production, distribution and consumption of symbols. In India, a similar development is taking place where "the fisherman's children" have become the producers of symbols, distributors and consumers for the software industry.

It is the simultaneous existence of disintegration and reintegration that leads to the global creative destruction in the new market, but which manifests itself locally, for instance, in a fishing village in Norway, or in a town in India (see "conceptualisation" in Figure 6).

The production costs of an industrial enterprise may be said to follow a certain logical pattern, i.e. they are distributed in modules in geographical areas where costs are low. The support (the back office) of an organisation may be said to follow a certain quality logic, and this is distributed in modules in geographical areas where the quality is high. The innovation and R&D department is likely to follow a creative logic. The head office is likely to follow an expertise and talent logic, and often be located in a large city. The cities of the world compete to provide the best knowledge workers (expertise in addition to talent) (see Normann, 2004: 297–300). Normann asks: "How can we become a good home for value creation activities" (ibid: 299). It is this question that cities need to answer if they are to attract knowledge workers and the head offices of major global businesses.

In its social consequences, what we have described above results in physical and geographical disintegration as well as virtual reintegration. When this type of logic manifests itself, most labour-intensive manufacturing will move to low-cost countries such as China (which is the tendency today) assuming that stable political structures continue. Support functions will be moved to places such as India (Bangalore), for instance, which is already the case to a certain extent. R&D and high-tech value creation activities will be moved to city areas that:

1. Have the necessary information structure
2. Have a competent creative environment with access to talent
3. Have relatively low costs for knowledge workers
4. Possess the necessary conditions for talent development

It is also important to note that low-cost countries such as China and India are also in the process of developing a highly skilled, talented and creative workforce; this means that so-called low-cost countries can now provide knowledge workers on relatively low salaries who are able to compete with knowledge workers in the West, who have relatively high salaries. Traditional trade theory, which expresses that the normalisation of trade occurs through the levelling of labour costs, will no longer be applicable because it does not necessarily apply in the global economy since there is such an incredibly large amount of low-cost labour available that can enter the various value creation processes.

The simultaneous existence of disintegration and reintegration processes characterizes the global market (Sennett, 2007, 2008). New patterns develop in which fundamental experiences collapse, resulting in needs, wants, preferences and expectations growing and becoming the basic indicators for action rather than demand. The time lag between the four abovementioned elements and demand constitutes the room for the field of innovation in global clusters of expertise. Innovation fields exist at various levels, and these are distributed in global clusters of expertise that operate physically in local contexts as well as in the global virtual space. We now move from the concretization in the conceptual diagram in Figure 5 to a new abstraction, which we illustrate in Figure 6.

Figure 6. The development of the field of innovation for high-tech value creation in global clusters of expertise

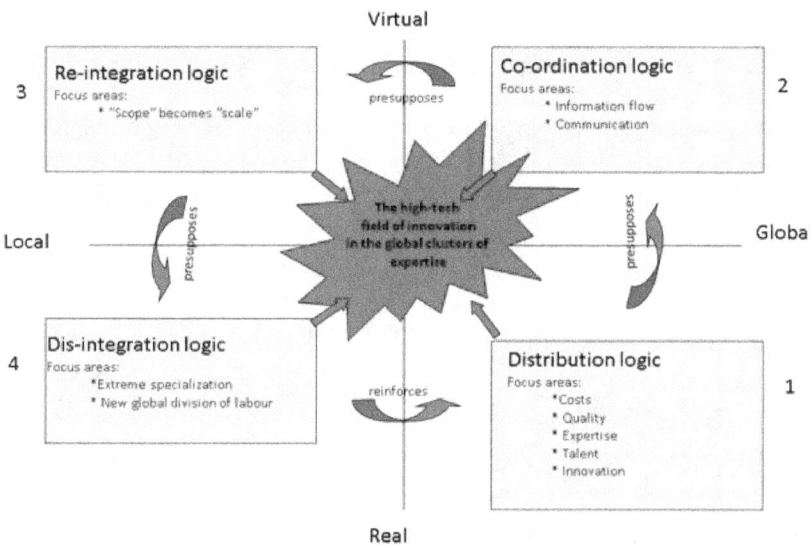

Conclusion

Theoretical consequences for individuals and organisations

The logic of distribution focuses on costs, quality, expertise, talent and innovation (Drucker, 1995; Kirzner, 1982). Consequently, various modules ("Lego organisations") for the functions of organisations in the global knowledge economy have been developed. The core processes and expertise of organisations are not left out of this logic of distribution, but they may be distributed in modules in global clusters of expertise.

The logic of coordination focuses on the flow of information and communication; consequently, ICT is essential for coordinating distributed Lego functions. The logic of reintegration triggers a classic paradox. Chandler (2004) points out that industrial enterprises could choose either scale or scope, but that something new has occurred in the global knowledge economy. Owing to Lego organisations, which the logic of distribution results in, and the opportunities for information flow and communication, which the logic of coordination results in, small, exclusive and unique can now be the economies of scale in the global market. Consequently, "scale" and "scope" are no longer two different domains, but rather prerequisites for each other's existence. Consequently, we say here that "scope" becomes "scale" in the global knowledge economy.

Reintegration leads to disintegration in the local sphere, where you often get an extreme level of specialisation. A new global division of labour is being developed, which reinforces and is reinforced by the logic of distribution's focus areas of costs, quality, expertise, talent and innovation (Sennett, 2007, 2008).

The development of the field of innovation (see Figures 4 and 6), both locally and globally, provides the sense of direction that is a necessary condition for high-tech value creation in the global knowledge economy.

With regard to such an innovation-driven economy, Hamel and Prahalad's (1996) ideas on the core processes are right and wrong at the same time. They are right in the sense that there will always be one or more core processes in various organisations. However, they are wrong in that these core processes can be atomised (modules), fragmented and distributed as numerous small Lego parts. Individually, these small Lego parts can develop in the global space and become viable entities. Similarly, the "cluster thinking" of Porter (1990: 131–179) and Breschi and Malerba (2007), among others, is also right and wrong at the same time. It is right in the sense that Breschi and Malerba (2007), among others, make it empirically apparent that economic growth and the development of innovations are promoted by local industrial clusters. For instance, consider industrial districts and high-tech regions such as Silicon Valley, Boston's biotechnology cluster and the Hsinchu–Taipei cluster (Taiwan). The point here is that these clusters are not necessarily geographically linked in so-called local clusters. In the global knowledge economy, both production and distribution are realised through global clusters of expertise. It will not be sufficient, even if it is not necessarily wrong, to develop policies for local industrial clusters. A policy for local clusters is only a necessary condition, not a sufficient condition for success in the global knowledge economy. The sufficient condition is at the same time developing a policy for global clusters of expertise, while the necessary and sufficient conditions trigger high-tech value creation because in the global knowledge economy, value creation, innovation and the transfer of experience occur as much in global clusters of expertise as they do in local clusters.

One of the results of high-tech value creation is not necessarily so-called virtual organisations (Hedberg et al., 2002), but rather a transformation of how organisations are structured away from traditional models to a structure similar to the way the market is organised. In other words, this is a form of modular flexibility that follows the logic of distribution, coordination, reintegration and disintegration, as illustrated in Figure 6.

Normann's (2004: 56) image of the same development is the "exploded company". This metaphor corresponds to our understanding of the Lego organisation of high-tech value creation. After the exploded company has fallen down, what is left? It is reasonable to assume that it rises from the ashes like a Phoenix in the form of modules distributed globally and held together by the logic of coordination and reintegration.

The social consequences are made apparent in the logic of disintegration, as shown by Sennett (2007, 2008) among others. Our point is that Normann's (2004) pieces become integrated into the market in which they fall down. Consequently, organised chaos emerges, termed here the field of innovation, which is connected through global clusters of expertise. These small exploded pieces begin to develop, but they have explosive dynamics built into them, which enables them to explode again, again and again, and glide into the market in which they fall down. However, the explosions and fallout areas are not random. They follow the five elements in the logic of distribution. We can expand Normann's image to be more like laser-guided small "cluster bombs" that, with surgical precision, both explode and fall down according to a specific logic. This offspring of Normann's exploded companies, in which we see the contours of high-tech value creation, is where the structures and processes implode in the market and become more or less integrated. At an abstract level, one can say that the production, distribution and consumption implode into each other in the global knowledge economy.

A growing market is not a precondition for the field of innovation, as Castells (2000) points out. The market and exploding modules merge in such a way that they become symbiotically linked and ultimately emerge as "the business of one and the market of one". Studies of what makes some businesses exceptional, as Peters (2004) shows, and some leaders exceptionally talented, as Collins (2001) and others point out, are not that relevant in the context of the global knowledge economy; such findings will become less valid because the explosions lead to the collapse of fundamental experiences. New requirements are emerging in the field of innovation, which is continually changing in relation to the four elements of logic shown in Figure 6.

It is reasonable to assume that organisations and leaders who survive such an explosive storm are those who will become one with their market. The individual modules will not become embedded into the market, but rather become immanent in the market, i.e. the market becomes the organisation.

Practical implications for leaders and organisations

The greater the pace of change, turbulence and complexity in the outside world, the less room there will be for planning for the future. However, we will always have knowledge about future developments. For instance, we know with great certainty that in the next 5–10 years the large *post-war Baby Boomer generation will reach retirement.* We know something about what will happen if the ice on the North and South Poles starts to melt. It is also known what will happen if a company is insolvent over a long period of time. It is not so much that our planning and strategic models will become useless, but rather that when the pace of change, turbulence and complexity increases, while fundamental experiences collapse, then the space where we can use such tools will become limited.

Simplified, one can relate to the outside world in two ways. One can adapt to changes in the outside world or one can create one's own future by influencing the outside world (see Ackoff, 1982). If the pace of change, turbulence and complexity increases, then the relevance of adapting to the outside world becomes less and it will be more appropriate to create one's own future.

Individuals with a high degree of intuition and understanding of patterns perceive that new developments are taking place; i.e. they become aware of emergent structures. Consequently, they situate themselves where the pattern manifests itself before it becomes evident as information. This means that they act on cues, signals and signs in the outside world. Then, by situating themselves and their organisations where the pattern eventually manifests itself, they will have secured a position from which they will be able to profit. In other words, they will be able to create their own and the organisation's future by taking advantage of the difference and time lag that exists between the cues, signals and signs (the little hints that something new is developing), on the one hand, and, the pattern that is realised in practice, on the other hand. When the pattern is realised, the gap in the market will soon be filled by other enterprises. However, in the meantime, large profits will have been made by those who acted based on these cues, signals and signs.

The emergent pattern first shows itself as a repetition of small signals and cues. After a while, these show themselves as successions, i.e., a particular pattern becomes stronger. When this pattern has manifested itself and shown itself as explicit knowledge, then everyone will have access to it. In other words, this does not concern "wild speculation", but rather disciplined, systematic and structured observations of the small signals and cues that underlie the actions that can result in making large profits in the global knowledge economy.

References

Ackoff, R.L. (1982). *Creating the corporate future: plan or be planned for*. Wiley, New York.

Adler, P. & Kwon, S.W. (2002). Social capital: prospects for a new concept. *Academy of Management Review, 27*, 17–40.

Audretsch, D.A. (2006). *Entrepreneurship, innovation and economic growth.* Edward Elgar Publishing, New York.

Bicak, K. (2005). *International knowledge transfer management.* Shaker Verlag, Aachen.

Breschi, S. & Malerba, F. (eds.). (2007). *Clusters, networks, and innovation*, Oxford University Press, Oxford.

Castells, M. (2000). *The rise of the network society.* Vol. 1, Blackwell, London.

Chandler, A.D. (2004). *Scale and scope: the dynamics of industrial capitalism.* Belknap Press, New York.

Collins, H.M. (1993). The structures of knowledge. *Social Research, 60,* 95–116.

Collins, J. (2001). *Good to great.* Random House, London.

Cooper, A.C. (1986). Entrepreneurship and high technology In Sexton, D.L. & Smilor, R.W. (Ed.). *The art and science of entrepreneurship*, Ballinger Publishing, Cambridge, Mas., pp. 153–167.

Drucker, P. F. (1995). *Managing in a time of great change.* Truman Talley Books, New York.

Drucker, P.F. (1999). *Management challenges for the 21st century*. Harper, New York.

Egan, G. (1977). *The skills of communicating and relating to each other*. Wadsworth, Belmont, CA.

Flynn, F.J., Chatman, J.A. & Spataro, S.E. (2001). Getting to know you. *Administrative Science Quarterly, 46,* 414–442.

.

Gilovich, T., Griffin, D. & Kahneman, D. (Ed.) (2002). *Heuristics and biases: the psychology of intuitive judgment*. Cambridge University Press, Cambridge.

Grant, R.M. (2003). The knowledge-based view of the firm, In Faulkner, D.O. & Campbell, A. *The Oxford Handbook of Strategy*, Oxford University Press, Oxford (pp. 203–231).

Gratton, L. (2002). *Living Strategy: putting people at the heart of corporate purpose*. Prentice Hall, New York.

Gratton, L. (2007). *Hot spots*. Prentice Hall, New York.

Hamel, G. & Prahalad, C.K. (1996). *Competing for the future*. Harvard Business School Press, Boston.

Handy, C. (1992). Balancing corporate power. *Harvard Business Review, 70*(6), 59–73.

Hedberg, B., Yakhlef, A. & Baumard, P. (2002). *Managing imaginary organizations: s new perspective on business*. Pergamon Press, London.

Hirooka, M. (2006). *Innovation dynamism and economic growth: a nonlinear perspective*. Edward Elgar Publishing, New York.

Jansen, W., Steenbakkers, W. & Jagers, H. (2007). *New business models for the knowledge economy*. Ashgate, New York.

Johannessen, J-A., Olaisen, J. & Olsen, B. (1999). Aspects of innovation theory based on knowledge management. *International Journal of Information Management 19(*2), 121–139

Kanter, R. M. (2006). From cells to communities: Deconstructing the organization, In Gallos, J.V. (Ed.). Organization development, Jossey Bass, San Francisco, pp. 858–888.

Kirzner, S. (1982). The theory of entrepreneurship in economic growth, In Kent, C.A., Sexton, D. L. & Vesper, K.H. (Ed.). *Encyclopedia of entrepreneurship*. Prentice Hall, Englewood Cliffs. N.J.

Kuhn, T. (2013). The Structure of scientific revolutions, University of Chicago Press, Chicago.

Lave, J. & Wenger, E.C. (1991). *Situated learning: legitimate peripheral participation.* Cambridge University Press, New York.

Lucia, S. (2004). *Contagious success.* Portfolio, New York.

Luhmann, N. (1996). *Social systems.* Stanford University Press, Stanford.

Nonaka, I. & Takeuchi, H. (1995). *The knowledge creating company.* Oxford University Press, Oxford.

Normann, R. (2004). *Reframing business: when the map changes the landscape.* John Wiley & Sons, New York.

North, D.C. (1990). Institutions, institutional change and economic performance, Cambridge University Press, Cambridge.

Peters, T. (2004). *In search of excellence.* Harper Business, London.

Pfeffer, J. & Sutton, I. (2000). *The knowing-doing gap.* Harvard Business School Press, Boston.

Polanyi, M. (1962). *Personal knowledge.* Routledge & Kegan Paul, London.

Polanyi, M. (1966). *The tacit dimension*. Gloucester, Mass.

Porter, M.E. (1990). *The competitive advantage of nations*. The Free Press, New York.

Rifkin, G. (1988). *The ultimate entrepreneur: the story of Ken Olsen and Digital Equipment Corporation*. Contemporary Books, Chicago.

Roberts, E. (1991). *Entrepreneurs in high technology*. Oxford University Press, Oxford.

Schumpeter, J.A. (1954). *History of economic analysis*. Oxford University Press, Oxford.

Sennett, R. (2007). *The culture of the new capitalism*. Yale University Press, New York.

Sennett, R. (2008). *The craftsman*. Allen lane, New York.

Strathdee, R. C. (2008). *Economic change, social networks and access to higher education in the 21st Century*, Palgrave Macmillan, New York.

Thakor, A.J. (2000). *Becoming a better value creator*. Jossey Bass, San Francisco.

Thurow, L.C. (2000). *Building wealth*. Collins, New York.

Tsoukas, H. & Shepherd, J. (2004). *Managing the future: foresight in the knowledge economy*. Blackwell Publishing, London.

Uzzi, B. (1997). Social structure and competition in interfirm networks: the paradox of embeddedness, *Administrative Science Quarterly, 42*, 35–67.

Vinton, D.E. (1992). Time, speed and the manager. *Academy of Management Executive, 6*, 7–16.

Waller, M., Conte, J., Gibsen, C. & Carpenter, M. (2001). The effect of individual perceptions of deadlines on team performance. *Academy of Management Review, 26*, 586–600.

Wenger, E.C., McDermott, R. & Snyder, W.H. (2002). *Communities of practice: a guide to managing knowledge*. Harvard Business School Press, Boston.

Werther Jr., W. & Chandler, D. (2005). *Strategic corporate social responsibility*. Sage, New York.

Chapter 3 Systemic Thinking, Knowledge and organizational innovations

Introduction

Systemic thinking has four main building blocks:

1. The subsystems and the system must be viewed in context, i.e. the part/whole relationship (Bateson, 1972: 437-438), which gives direction for stability and structure.

2. The system in the environment, not the system separated by a border is emphasised (Luhmann, 1995, Bunge, 1997: 415), which gives direction for identity and norms.

3. The element-relation connection (Bunge, 1996; 1997) which gives direction for changes in the system.

4. The reorganisation of the system of relations (Luhmann, 1995), which give direction for creation processes and innovation in the system.

In systemic thinking (Bunge, 1983; 1983a; 1985; 1985a; 1996; 1997), an important question is: What is the pattern which combines a given phenomenon or problem? (Bateson, 1972: 130-134). The noticeable thing about patterns is that it is difficult to pinpoint cause and effect, i.e. there is a tacit dimension involved. A pattern can metaphorically be regarded as a circle or a spiral, and a circle has no beginning or end. The pattern is connected by relationships, and :» the relationship of the particulars jointly forming a whole may be ineffable, even though all the particulars are explicitly specifiable» (Polanyi, 1958: 88). This means that the tacit dimension is an important coefficient in patterns, especially regarding organisations as social systems.

The systemic angle of incidence requires the study of social systems to consist of four subsystems: the biological, the cultural, the economic, and the political (Bunge, 1985; 1996).

For the biological subsystem it is social relationships between persons which constitute its media. For the cultural subsystem it is values which constitute its media. For the economic subsystem it is material artefacts and money which constitute its media. For the political subsystem it is power which constitute its media. If one of the four subsystems is studied, then, in the systemic angle of incidence, critical variables from the other three subsystems must not be taken for granted exogenously, but be a part of the model subject to study. Every subsystem must learn to regard itself from an external perspective relative to the three other subsystems. This is of course controversial, but is a main argument by

Bunge (1985), and by Polanyi (1958; 1962; 1966). We also find support for this argument by Luhmann (1982; 1986; 1990; 1992).

One set of reasons based on the systemic point of view for including all these variables in the study of social systems, is provided by Bunge (1992:39): "All systems-----receive input and are selective, that is they react only to the subset of the totality of environmental actions impinging them." To try to overcome this selective section, one could e.g. explore the possibility of analysing the study of each social system and include variables from the four subsystems constituting a social system from a systemic point of view.

In what follows I will define some concepts used in the chapter, not to achieve any strict definitions, but to explain the terms I use as interpretative devices for the reader:

Function: When using the concept function, we are referring to Myrdal's (1944:1056) understanding: "The term function can have a meaning only in terms of an assumed purpose." Rephrased it can be formulated in a question: In what way does the function contribute to the maintenance (possibly change) of what the system is meant to accomplish (i.e. the purpose)?

Three types of knowledge will be defined in the following:

Explicit knowledge: Explicit knowledge is here understood as the part of knowledge which can be verbally communicated to others as information.

Tacit knowledge: The tacit part of our knowledge, says Polanyi (1962), is the part linked to skills not easily communicated by means of information, e.g. the act of explaining to others how other people's glances are to be interpreted in a situation.

Hidden knowledge: Hidden knowledge is here defined as the part of knowledge which structures our premises, suppositions, prerequisites and motives. The fact that this knowledge is hidden makes it difficult for us to realise what determining factors are involved in our actions or attitudes. If this part of knowledge remains more or less hidden, conflicts can easily ensue without any corresponding knowledge on our part as to how and why they occur. We find support for this concept "hidden knowledge" in Schutz' (1990, Vol. 1 and 2.) "epoche" concept.

Cybernetics is: "a way of reasoning in the sciences" (Popovic, 1962: iii). Wiener (1947) expands the concept cybernetics in his second edition of his book to include self-organising and self-producing systems. Through this understanding of cybernetics the autopoiesis theory is directly linked to the system-theoretical tradition in science. Bateson's idea about "the external mind" (1988) can also be seen as a link to the autopoiesis theory. It was in fact the pattern of relations tying a system together into a coherent structure which occupied Bateson as an idea.

A continued development of classical cybernetic thinking, with its emphasis on management, control, and communication, has been carried out by sociocybernetics. The concept was developed by Geyer & Van der Zouwen (1978). Sociocybernetics can be defined as: "the application of concepts, methods, and ideas of the so-called new cybernetics or second-order cybernetics to the study of social and sociocultural systems". (Geyer & Van der Zouwen, 1992:95).

While classical cybernetics or first-order cybernetics is based on positivism, second-order cybernetics is more actor-oriented and focuses on the observer observing the social system. The misconception that systems theory is exclusively oriented towards first-order cybernetics was already discussed by Von Bertalanffy (1973:15). In sociocybernetics there is now a clear distinction between the philosophy of science of first-order cybernetics, and second-order cybernetics respectively.

The question asked is: In what way can systemic thinking be used as a means to understand, explain and predict stability and change in organisations regarded as social systems? The chapter is organised as follows: First we describe and discusses normative open and cognitive closed systems in relation to autopoiesis theory. Then we analyse the normative superstructure and the normatively closed loop. We describe information capital and the cognitively open loop.

Normative open and cognitive closed

«It has been authoritatively stated that the moment of greatest creative advancement in science frequently coincide with the introduction of new notions by means of a definition» (Polanyi, 1958: 189). This also applies to cybernetics and autopoiesis.

Autopoiesis means self-producing system. Autopoiesis theory was developed by Maturana & Varela (1980). Luhmann introduces the distinction between normatively closed and cognitively open systems at the social level (Luhmann, 1975). An autopoietic social system with this distinction is simultaneously closed (normatively) and open (cognitively). The normative and the cognitive are also structurally linked, generating interaction between these two subsystems. A crucial point here is: "closure is a condition for openness" (Luhmann, 1986:183). It is among other things the link between the normatively closed and the cognitively open which is Luhmann's contribution to the autopoietic theory for social systems, and which creates organisational innovation at the theory and design level for organisations.

The cognitive openness is a form of awareness or knowledge link to the environment of the system, which maintains organisational learning. The recursive element is critical for the understanding of the normative element at various recursivity levels.

It must be emphasised that the "normative"-loop also is open in a sense, though with a longer time lag than the "cognitive"-loop. One example is the development of the Catholic church.

For the individual system there exists a system-specific normative basis. At a superior recursivity level there is also a normative superstructure in evidence, influencing the normative basis for the subordinate recursivity level. The normative basis at the recursivity level above the individual system-specific normative basis, is here called the normative superstructure. This must not be interpreted as the misunderstood idea that there is one single normative superstructure. Every system is connected to its own normative superstructure, but this is not the point made here. The point is that systems operating in an organizational field (Johannessen, 1996) have the same normative superstructure, structuring the behaviour of the whole field of organisations. The normative superstructure for each field is linked to other normative superstructures in other organizational fields, possibly but only possibly emerging into an emergent new normative superstructure for the domain of an integrated organizational field on a higher recursivity level. But, there certainly is no single normative superstructure in the world as a whole. This would have excluded the knowledge gained so far in cybernetics, and maybe been the beginning of the end for mankind.

The study of social systems as autopoietic systems, according to Luhmann (1986:186):" is a theory of self-referential systems, to be applied to observing systems as well". This links social autopoiesis theory to second-order cybernetics, as expressed by Heinz Von Foerster (1981), among others. For the individual researcher it becomes just as much a question of self-observation as observation of the social system. It is self-reflection which Luhmann and von Foerster bring in as a point. Luhmann (1986:187) says: "To combine these two distinctions (between autopoiesis and observation, and between external observation and self-observation, our inclusion) is one of the unsolved tasks in systems theory". The core of the problem as we see it is that an observer observing a social system constitutes an autopoietic system in his own right, i.e. when we gather information about social systems we cannot avoid collecting information about ourselves. Luhmann (1986:188) points out that in order to solve this problem (paradox) a sort of exchange between external observation and self-observation is required. One possible strategy could be for the observer to make his assumptions, premises and suppositions explicit (the explication principle). The actors will through this process make their norm and value basis explicit for themselves.

Ulrich (1983;1986;1987;1988) also directs his attention towards suppositions, the normative content on the part of the observer, and the consequences for those affected by the products of a system in the "Critical Systems Heuristic" concept. Ulrich particularly emphasises the question: What should be done? instead of the instrumental question: How is it done. It is Ulrich's position that the freedom of choice is also a type of critical freedom to reflect on ourselves as observers and system designers which Polanyi (1958, 1962) also emphasise.

The system-specific normative basis, regardless of its being based on a model-weak foundation (Bråten, 1984), generates an attention focus in the system. The system-specific normative basis influence and set standards for signals, symbols and the information to be selected, in addition to the expectations on the part of the individual actors in the system. This in turn produces certain experiences in the system, which then reinforce or sustain the system-specific foundation. This is what we here refer to as information capital. Understood this way relationships are build and rebuild by controlling the system-specific normative basis

If it is so that what we know depends on how we got to know it

(Watzlawick, 1984:9), a continuos examination of explications pertaining to one's own way of thinking becomes essential, for taking control of ones way of thinking, and not being controlled by the system-specific normative basis.

Luhmann emphasises communication as the very foundation for social systems. Luhmann's conceptual pairings (normatively closed and cognitively open) make it possible for a social system to be simultaneously self-producing in terms of social norms, and still maintain the capability of learning, through the cognitive openness of the system. Luhmann (199:12) points out: " the concept of autopoietic closure has to be understood as the recursively closed organisation of an open system". The point is the extent to which normative closure and cognitive openness exists in a specific system. It is, according to Luhmann (1990: 13), communication which constitutes the evolutionary potential for the construction of systems able to "maintain closure under the condition of openness". It is Ashby's (1968) definition of the cybernetic system which Luhmann seems to use as basis for his use of the autopoiesis theory in his study of Germany's legal system: "the legal system is open to cognitive information but closed to normative control" (Luhmann, 1990:229). Ashby's (1968:4) expression of the cybernetic system is: "Open to energy but closed to information and control". Even if the system is closed normatively, it does not follow that it is not subject to influences from the outside world. An autopoietical system is openly cognitive, and can therefore both influence other systems and at the same time learn and adapt to the outside world. Organisational learning and innovation are thereby linked to the cognitively open loop.

An autopoietic social system is, in other words, both open and closed at the same time. There is openness towards the outside world, starting as internal reflection, redefinition of situations and generation of communication.

The normative closure is secured by means of a number of mechanisms preventing information and communication from the outside from penetrating the system. Examples of such mechanisms could be: laws, rules, regulations, routines, tribal language, i.e. the concepts, theories and axioms of various professions. In turn these mechanisms can be constituted by standards, i.e. expectations and notions from economic, social, political and cultural systems of the outside world.

The epistemological consequence of social autopoiesis theory for a researcher on social systems is that he refers to himself when studying these systems. The researcher must be aware of this self-reference and problematize it. Otherwise the study of social systems will become a self-reference study regardless of method. This makes the subjective element a focal point in the study of social systems (Polanyi, 1958). The reflection concerning one's own understanding is also important for Luhmann. Or according to Geyer & Van der Zouwen (1992:102): "Within a society, all observations are by definition self-observations". One consequence of this is that the observer, the observer's statements and the problem or phenomenon subject to study, are three separate elements subject to evaluation in the study of social systems.

There is not any agreement as to whether social systems can be regarded as autopoietical systems. Luhmann (1982;1986) and Robb (1989;1989a) argues in favour of the contention that the theory can be adapted to social systems. Maturana (1981), Varela (1979) and Mingers (1989) have more doubt about the fruitfulness of this analogy. Our view is that autopoietic processes can be disclosed as parallel processes, not identical, in social systems and organisations. By this we mean that knowledge based on the autopoiesis theory at the cell level with Maturana and Varela, can be adapted for the purpose of acquiring knowledge of social processes in organisations regarded as social systems. This we also interpret as Luhmann's point of view (1986:173). Luhmann's application of the autopoiesis theory can be used to describe, explain and possibly predict change or lack of change in social systems. Luhmann's autopoiesis understanding is neither a conflict model nor a consensus model, but an evolution model.

The normative superstructure has relations to more systems and thus more system-specific bases than indicated in figure 1, i.e. the normative superstructure is linked to the entire field (Johannessen, 1996) of which the specific system is part.

By norms in the model, we here mean: "Norms thus have, above all the function of integrating the needs of operating units with each other and reconciling them with the needs of the system as a whole.---. Norms spell out expectations for collectives and for persons acting in roles, and in doing so, may bring to light discrepancies among these expectations" (Parsons, 1967:155).

The system-specific normative basis constitutes the starting point for the development of identity on the part of the system, i.e. how the system understands itself. The loop between the normative superstructure and the system-specific normative basis is a protective loop for the field being conservative in nature.

Through self-observation in the system, and reflection on itself and in relation to other systems, learning and innovation can take place. This is the right side of the model, which reflects the cognitive opening of the system. The loop between the cognitive opening and the environment is an opening for learning, here referred to as the learning loop.

The normative superstructure and the system-specific normative basis have a mutually conservative effect, which hinders innovation. The cognitive open loop on the other hand, adds requisite variety to the system, which promotes innovation and organisational learning.

Selection processes (signals, symbols, information), the expectation mechanism and the experience dimension in the normatively closed loop, constitute what we here denote as the information capital of the system, reproducing the system-specific normative basis, and being linked to tacit knowledge.

The construct information capital states that it is basic experience which to a great extent determines the selection mechanisms we utilise and the expectations determining our behaviour. The selection processes and the expectations then reinforce and sustain the basic experiences and the system-specific normative basis. Tacit knowledge in this way thus function as a conservative element. Small differences pertaining too the starting point for basic experiences can through dynamic and self-reinforcing processes generate great differences both in terms of selection processes and expectations. It is the system-specific normative basis which functions as a damper mechanism on these potentially self-reinforcing mechanisms and thus stabilises the system.

The reflection possibility and the variation potential are both firmly rooted in the cognitively open loop, both internally in the model element and in the opening to other systems, and function as the learning and innovative element. The internal variation potential is contingent on the actors reflecting on their own value basis or the system-specific normative basis. We here make a distinction between the value system and the system-specific normative basis. The value system (Johannessen, 1997) is constituted by the needs and legitimate wishes on the part of the actors. "Values,---, I understand to be conceptions of the desirable, applies to various objects and standing at various levels of generality". (Parsons, 1967:147). The values being ingrained in needs and legitimate wishes is also explicitly expressed by Bunge (1989). The system-specific normative basis is the norm of the system in relation to the function the system is meant to fulfil. The norms have their functions in terms of sustaining the system of relations between positions in the field, as tacit knowledge functions in its consequences as a conservative element.

The purpose of the cognitive openness is to increase the sensibility, connectivity and receptivity on the part of the system towards the world, and thus be linked to selected parts of this world. Through communication with the environment the awareness of the actors in the system is developed. When the actors in turn reflect on this awareness and introduce this communicatively to the system, irritation and/or tension towards the system-specific normative basis is easily generated, further reinforcing the communication in the system.

The normative superstructure and the normatively closed loop.

The normative superstructure and the system-specific normative basis generate a certain habitus (Bourdieu, 1992), i.e. patterns of thought and action dispositions on the part of the actors. The thought and action dispositions are contingent on how the actors have organised their knowledge. Their experiences are generated through the use of knowledge and reinforce the suppositions of the actors, due to expectations seen in the light of signals, symbols and the information being selected in the system. The selection processes to a certain extent precipitate the events to be expected (See Thomas theorem in Merton, 1968: 20).

When using the concepts the normative super-structure and the system-specific normative basis, there are no unambiguous definitions to be deduced from the concepts. In order to clarify these concepts, we shall borrow three concepts from Bourdieu: Social field, symbolic capital and habitus.

By social field is meant a system of relations between positions occupied by special agents and institutions fighting for what they have in common (Broady, 1991:17). The field concept is a system of relations between positions (Broady, 1991:462). The position is indicated by means of position and location in the social room. The field concept can be seen as a breakdown of the role concept. While the role concept focuses on expectations directed towards certain roles, the field concept focuses on relations between positions. The field concept of Bordieu becomes a tool suitable for the disclosure of the normative super-structure and the system-specific normative basis. Every system becomes aware of its norms, according to Bordieu, by relating them to the norms of other groups (Broady, 1991:463).

Symbolic capital is everything recognised as valuable by the social group (Broady, 1991:462). Habitus is the system of dispositions permitting human beings to think, act, and orient themselves in the social world (Broady, 1991:12). The habitus concept tries to link the subjective and the objective in the social room (Broady, 1991:453).

To disclose the normative superstructure and the system-specific normative basis the focus will have to be put on relations between actors in central positions. The question will then be: What system of relationships exists? Systems of relationships can e.g. revolve around:

Dominance relationships, access to resources, opinions regarding social problems, investments in knowledge, types of conversion strategies, networks available, relations to other fields, instances of symbolic access and material access, value hierarchy, access rules and geographical location of the positions. It is in particular the relation properties pertaining to Bourdieu's concepts which make them conducive to systemic thinking. Systemic thinking emphasises relations between elements more than the substance of the individual elements. This is one of the basic prerequisites for the study of social systems, from a systemic point of view. The precedence of relations is also rooted in all cybernetic understanding of phenomena and problems. This is stated in Ashby (1961;1968;1970;1981), Bateson (1972;1988) and Bunge (1983; 1983a; 1985; 1985a). This is where systemic thinking and Bourdieu's project display close parallels. The relations and their system character is a central aspect of Bourdieu's sociology, according to Broady (1991:464). On the basis of this line of thinking isolating single factors and e.g. establishing connections between them would give the wrong idea. It is the entire system of relations generating a phenomenon which should constitute the ambitions in terms of disclosure on the part of research, or alternatively patterns of interactions over a period of time.

On the basis of the previous discussion, we can enlist certain criteria for the study of the normative super-structure and the system-specific normative basis:

1. Patterns: Social relationships between actors generate certain patterns of thought and action positions in the social field.

2. Distinction: The action pattern differs from the other action positions in other social fields.

3. Unity: The action pattern is shared by the actors in the social field.

4. Autopoiesis: The action pattern reproduces itself through the norms.

For the actors in the individual system it will be difficult to see that the normative basis impacts their action dispositions. They will also find it difficult to disclose this basis, as it is their own system behaviour which sustains and reinforces it. From the actor's point of view it may appear that he is relatively autonomous and free in the sense that he has the possibility to develop his own solutions to problems likely to appear. But the behaviour is only instrumental in sustaining established action positions, and the freedom is therefore only relative in relation to the actions allowed by the normative superstructure.

The norms are institutionalised through the development of the system of relations between the actors, who in turn constitute the stability of the social system. The systems of relation is critical, as they develop a reciprocity between the actors and thus penetrate the entire system or major parts of it.

It is the system of relations and interactions in its entirety which constitutes the normative superstructure, not the individual persons or institutions in this network. There is a structural link between the normative super-structure and the system-specific basis. Structural linking in this context means: "whenever there is a history of recurrent interactions leading to the structural congruence between two or more systems" (Maturana & Varela, 1987:75).

One major purpose of the normative super-structure viewed in this context, is to ascertain that the change in the individual system is not carried out more rapidly than what will allow for the complete structure to make the necessary adjustment. If this should happen, the entire field could collapse. One such change could be regarded as a morpho-genetic change, i.e. as change affecting the entire system and possibly the organisational fields and generating new relations between the elements allowing new structures and power constellations to occur, i.e. innovation in social systems. Changes not affecting the whole system, allowing new relations, structures and power constellations to occur, are here called morphostatic changes. The normative superstructure is to ascertain that morphostatic changes take place, while preventing morphogenetic changes.

Structural innovations happen:

1. Through the normative superstructure undergoing morphogenetic changes, or

2. through the cognitive open system influencing the system-specific basis in a manner conducive to the normative superstructure undergoing morphogenetic changes.

The normative superstructure influences the system-specific normative basis, among other things, through its model power (see Bråten, 1973; 1984; 1986). Bråten (1986:193) defines a socio-cultural system as: "a meaning processing system interacting participants who maintain and transform the identity of themselves and their network through a more or less shared understanding of both themselves and of their network through a more or less shared understanding of both themselves and the world". Under certain circumstances, according to Bråten (1986:193), the shared common notions are "closed to a degree that rules out any rival view---. Such a system state may be called a model monopoly". Bråten's concept model monopoly is here linked directly to the normative superstructure in fig. 1. The normative superstructure in one field differs from the other normative superstructures in other fields by virtue of its values, identity, and model monopoly.

Proposition 1: The more model-strong the actors are, the greater is their control of their own situation, and the easier it will be for them to change the system according to their own interests.

While we here use Bourdieu's (1984;1988; 1992) focus on the system of relations between positions to describe the normative super-structure, Bråten (1973;1984) in his model monopoly concept focuses on the concrete actors in the field, who by virtue of being model-strong also induce other actors to reflect their interests and perspectives. There is no contradiction between Bråten's perspectives and ours; only a disclosure of different aspects of the normative super-structure.

Proposition 2: When tensions and conflicts occur between the system-specific norm and practice, it may be expressed as a conflict between various types of model application.

Morphostatic changes are necessary in order to maintain the stability and flexibility of the total system. This stability and flexibility is constituted through a constant disorganising process (see Johannessen, 1994). This is also expressed with Robb (1992:156) who states that morphogenetic changes: "involve redefining the models of reality held in view in the organisation--".

The normative superstructure has direct and subtle evaluation patterns for control of the individual systems. The subtle instrument is constituted by values and norms transferred and maintained in various ways, e.g. through ceremonies, education, ideas, symbols, and the formation of opinion. The direct control system is more linked to rules and regulations. Both the direct and the subtle control mechanisms are differentiated and vague and thus relatively difficult to catch sight of for an observer of such systems.

The system-specific norms are carriers of the normative super-structure in the same manner (analogy) as a context conveying messages, where the superstructure is analogue with the context.

Every system-specific normative basis in a social field to a certain extent reflects the normative superstructure. I.e. the normative superstructure is recursively present in all system-specific normative bases, like a holographic representation. Through the norms the system reproduces itself, and it is here that self-production and the autopoietic point enter the model (figure 1).

The normative superstructure or the system-specific normative basis can rarely be disclosed through the study of individuals and their influence, despite the fact that such case studies do exist (see Rød Larsen, 1976). It is the system of relations between positions which constitutes the super-structure, and the interaction between the persons which occupies these positions. The relation between the normative superstructure and the system-specific normative basis represents two different logical orders, where the normative superstructure takes precedence over the system-specific normative basis.

The normative superstructure is constituted and developed through specific formal procedures, e.g., legislation, common education, network contacts inside and outside the specific educational institutions and positions in society. The normative superstructure in this way constitutes a normatively closed system of relations. It can not necessarily legitimate itself, but will be legitimated through direct and indirect influences towards the system-specific normative basis, through e.g. model power. More direct power determinations could be: limited resource allocations to specific types of projects within a specific system, limitations in career opportunities etc. It is in other words not a matter of programming of the underlying systems relative to the normative superstructure, but a more or less voluntary internalisation of the normative superstructure which in turn will impact the entire field.

The normative superstructure is in most fields so firmly established that it is in no need to legitimise its hierarchical position through the primitive means outlined above, due to their becoming universally accepted truths. Inherent is the germ of collapse for this superstructure or, the breakthrough for the specific normative basis. The hypothesis is that the system which does not continuously reflect on its normative basis, will be exposed to intruders with strong models.

Information capital

Information capital is here defined as the interaction between expectation, experiences and the selection processes operating in a system. This may be seen as tacit components in Polanyi's (1958, 1966) concept of tacit knowledge, i.e. the 'praxical' grasp of the structure of the situation.

Our expectations related to a person will influence our reaction to his behaviour. If, e.g., we have the impression that such a person can be trusted, then our behaviour towards this person will be qualitatively affected by this impression. If, on the contrary, another impression has been created as far as this person is concerned, through rumours etc., our behaviour towards this person will be completely different. But it is more serious than that. Our behaviour towards the person will reinforce the behaviour to be expected from this person. Rumours and prejudices in this way become mechanisms conducive to the expected behaviour, and our previous "knowledge" is thus confirmed so to speak, i.e. the tacit component functions as a conservative element. This mechanism applies regardless of the actual truth value in our expectations. The first person to make scientific reports about this phenomenon in human interaction was Kelly (1950). In this way expectations towards another person carry an impact in themselves.

According to the model on expectation value by Fischbein & Ajzen (1975), we are supposed to attach to the reference object a certain expected subjective probability for occurrence. A reference object is the object to which the actual information is related. At the same time we attach certain values, positive and negative, to the qualities of the reference object. Our attitude to the reference object is then the sum of our expectations multiplied by the values attached to it.

The point in this context is that it is fair to assume that the information supporting our attitudes to the reference object will have more cognitive authority than information conflicting with our attitudes. We find support for this assumption with Sheppard, Hartwich & Warshaw (1988). Implications for a social system, will be that the flexibility and the innovation capacity of the system is greater if we actively seek information going against our expectations.

McGuire (1985) criticises the expectation model, stating, among other things, that there is a possibility that the model only deals with just a few properties of the reference object. But this does not budge our assumption that there is a strong link between one's own attitudes and the cognitive authority of the information which the reference object carries for us. What we do with this information is another thing, i.e. if it drives us to action or not.

For Luhmann it is the system in the environment which constitutes a central magnitude in the study of social systems. Social processes can then be analysed with regard to their function in terms of reducing the complexity towards the environment. An important point with Luhmann's theory is that he regards the increasing complexity on the part of society as a central point in the development of it. One way of reducing the complexity according to Luhmann is for the system to assume certain clear and stable expectations towards the environment. The expectations are divided in two categories by Luhmann:

1. The actual expectations, i.e. the ones that can be changed if they turn out to be wrong. This constitutes the learning dimension of an expectation.

2. The normative expectations, which is sustained regardless of their being fulfilled. Normative expectations are linked to a long time horizon, i.e. they sustain themselves over a very long time. They are further linked to the content dimension, i.e. they express general types of action patterns as desirable. Finally they are linked to a social institutionalisation dimension, i.e. the expectations are accepted by actors who perform a profession, e.g. the doctors at a hospital.

Proposition 3: Social systems to a great extent sustain their stability through normative expectations.

As far as the individual system and the partial system in a social field are concerned, they have relative freedom to experiment within the limitations of actual expectations. Within the normative expectations there is a hierarchy, on the other hand, where the system at the lower level must be adjusted according to systems at a higher level. It is, however, the normative superstructure which determines the actions to be performed by the individual actor in the individual system. This means in concrete terms that if the actions in the systems are developed in such a way that the power basis of the superstructure is threatened, the hierarchy will intervene in order to reinstate the original order. In this way the normative superstructure will restore its model monopoly. It has to be added, however, that in the practical every-day life all systems in all fields are to a certain extent equal from the beginning, i.e. in terms of profession the individual actors in principle have the same impact potential, but in conflict situations with the normative superstructure, the latter has normative penetrative power. There are two reasons for this: Firstly a higher degree of legitimacy has been attributed to the normative superstructure in society, and secondly, and the most important point here, the normative superstructure have more or less direct links to other normative superstructures (in the model the indicator between the superstructure and environment), in society. Through such a system of relations to other normative superstructures the normative superstructure will be in a position to impact the system-specific normative basis. Insofar as legitimacy and the model monopoly of the normative superstructure is threatened, the field-protection mechanism will be activated, and system innovation will be hindered.

The cognitively open loop.

Problem definition and framing the situation in the model (fig. 1) is closely linked to the Thomas theorem: "If men define situations as real, they are real in their consequences" (Merton, 1968: 20). How we define a situation or the boundaries for what we can and cannot do thus becomes critical for the behaviour in social systems displayed by the actors.

It is the manner in which knowledge is developed and sustained which can constitute our access to understanding and using Luhmann's conceptual postulate. Luhmann can be seen in the light of a functionalistic development of Parsons and Merton as some of the influential sources. Luhmann is however very critical towards Parsons action theory and emphasises communication as the central starting point for an analysis of social systems. In relation to Merton, Luhmann distances himself from the emphasis on empirical proximity, of which Merton has been a strong supporter.

Communication is the basic constituent in social systems, according to Luhmann (1986:176): "Social systems use communications as their particular mode of autopoietic reproduction,---. Communication is not actions. Their unity requires a synthesis of three selections; namely information, utterance and understanding(including misunderstanding)." Communication occurs, among other things, as a consequence of irritation , as, says Luhmann (1995:79 - 92; 1992) the awareness is located in the environment. There is a close connection here to Bateson's concept "the external mind". Luhmann further emphasises (1990:86-87) that communication is the smallest constituent in social interaction: "Without communication there can be no human relations". Luhmann (1990:6) further underlines his criticism of Parsons action theory by making the following comment: "Therefore, the theory of autopoietic social systems requires a conceptual revolution within sociology: the replacement of action theory by communication theory as characterisation of the elementary operative level of the system."

To express communication as e.g. "speech acts" or "Kommunikative-handelen" is for Luhmann to reduce communication to one of its possible consequences, or, according to Luhmann (1986:178): "Above all communication is not a kind of action, because it always contains a far richer meaning than the utterance or transmittance of the message only." Here we expand Luhmann's communication knowledge by splitting up a message in three parts: the information part, which in Luhmann's terminology is an "utterance"; the relation part and the hierarchy part

(Johannessen, 1995, Johannessen & Hauan, 1994). By looking at communication only as speech acts, many aspects of the transmission and translation will fall outside the communication analysis.

Communication presupposes an understanding on the part of the actors of both code and context, in addition to adequate attention relative to the purpose of communication. For the participants of the interaction system it is not possible to non-communicate (Luhmann, 1990: 88).

Communication, according to Luhmann (1990:13): "is an evolutionary potential for building up systems that are able to maintain closure under the condition of openness".

The interaction between actors links communication to an action category. But interaction is also linked to the hierarchy part in a message. The interaction of a system must also "take into account environmental communication" (Luhmann, 1986:177). This is the learning loop shown in figure 1, which constitutes the innovation potential between the system and the environment.

The relationships between individuals are constituted and further developed through communication. Their communication can in its consequence lead to certain actions, but analytically there is a major distinction between communication and action.

Communication is not only part of an interaction and action system. Communication is included even more in a translation- and meaning-generative system. An attempt to display this mechanism figuratively is made in figure 1.

Figure 1 Communication: An abstract vizualization

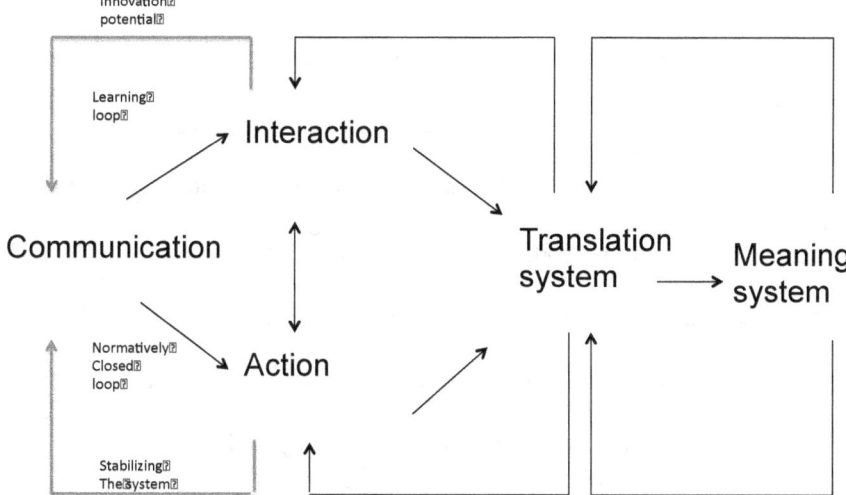

Communication also operates in the normatively closed loop, and is thus the most important change mechanism in the entire system. Communication is the mechanism bringing the various types of awareness in the system together. The awareness in the system finds its "closure" through communication, while it is the norms which constitute the stabilising element in the system.

Proposition 4: Communication constitutes and changes interaction, action, translation, meaning and the normative basis in social systems.

Actions can be a consequence of communication, but not necessarily. Communication and action occur at different logical levels, and a mixture can easily lead to confusion of the other consequences and functions of communication, e.g. translation and meaning. Communication can bring forth both the tacit knowledge and the hidden knowledge inherent in the system, and in this fashion change the normative basis, completely or partially. Luhmann (1986:179) expresses: "The distinction of communication and action----are operative requirements". We should add that they are analytical distinctions which in the empirical context may appear to intermingle, but still exist at different logical levels, and thus be subject to separation for analytical purposes.

Problem definition

Social systems transcend their normative closure by redefinition of boundaries and thereby give new meaning to the system through communication and self-reflection.

When the system reflects itself and its environment, the learning element has been introduced into the system (the learning loop in figure 1). Luhmann (1975, volume 2:73) describes this process as system rationality. It is in fact by reflecting on, and gradually making one's own self-reference explicit, that the normative basis can be changed and organisational innovation can be developed. It is in this way we here interpret Luhmann's rationality concept (Luhmann, 1975, volume 5).

The purpose of the problem definition is the establishment of a complete survey of the boundaries to be established, the context the problem has been subject to, and the relations between the parts of the problem and the whole (systemic structuring). Another purpose is that when a situation is defined or redefined, our attitudes are also organised towards the situation, and learning and innovation may occur.

Where we draw up the boundaries is not a trivial matter. A slight rephrasing of the Thomas theorem could be as follows: A situation will in its consequence be a result of where we draw up the boundaries for the problem/phenomenon. Luhmann (1986:176) expresses some of the same idea by saying: "By communication they extend and limit the social system, deciding about whether and what to communicate".

To a major extent it is where we through communication draw up the boundaries for a phenomenon or a problem which in its consequence will influence our perception of the phenomenon or the problem (in fig. 4 as two separate systems or as two overlapping systems). This may also be seen as the punctuation process in communication, i.e. it is our boundaries or distinctions which will constitute the basis for further communication. The introduction of boundaries could easily change communication in terms of form and structure, which could hinder/promote innovation depending on the punctuation of the communication process.

One important point of problem definition is that our picture of the environment is instrumental in our decision regarding the definition of a problem, situation etc.

It is in this connection important to underline that we as observers are one part of the social setting, and that we consequently influence the situation through our way of defining the problem or situation. We do not, then, stand outside the problem, as observers, watching it. In social interaction we are always a part of what we observe. This distinction is critical. We are not observers, but rather part of what we observe, and this makes problem definition extremely difficult. If we are not aware of this, we will often find ourselves in a conflict situation towards our expectations regarding what we believe to be our object for observation. One can not create social reality in the same manner as a carpenter makes a chair. We are part of what is being created and thus subject to change during the process. There is mutual interaction between us as observers of the social reality and the social reality itself.

Any problem denotes a borderline towards another problem, but all problems collectively are part of the superior situation. How we structure a problem and where we draw up the boundaries for the problem will thus affect the entire situation, and will give direction for identity, stability, change and innovation processes in the system.

The authentical situation, i.e. where one is honest towards oneself and the other(s), where co-operation, trust and a helping attitude exist, will, among other things, make parts of tacit and hidden knowledge accessible for explicit knowledge (see Judge et .al. 1997, Peck, 1985; Borei, 1992, Senge, 1990), and thus potentially accessible for communication and in this way promote organisational-learning and- innovation. If this should happen, we will, when a problem is being structured, develop an awareness of the premises and assumptions controlling our definitions and delineation's of a problem in a situation.

Proposition 5: Tacit knowledge and hidden knowledge is affecting the structuring of problems.

The boundaries of a phenomenon or a problem must always be drawn according to our purposes. Where we set the limits of a problem is not a trivial matter. It is critical to the outcome of our asking questions, regardless of the fact that the same question for the same phenomenon or problem may be asked. It is in other words the way in which a problem is defined which gives many of the premises for the solutions themselves.

The fact that persons draw up the boundaries of a problem in different ways can be explained through three underlying mechanisms (Bandler and Grinder, 1975):

A. We generalise from reality.

B. We select something and select out something else.

C: We make distortions and changes of which we are not aware.

It is fair to assume that the same processes which are operative when we draw up the boundaries of a problem, also are active when we communicate to others how the problem is to be understood.

1. We generalise on the basis of personal experiences

2. We choose selectively from our memory to a great extent, and

3. We distort, or are creative in relation to our memory, making a distorted relation to what has

   been stored originally.

This could be denoted as "the fallacy of information" and leads to the following proposition.

Proposition 6: Interpretation of information will be distorted due to the need for sustaining previous experiences.

Proposition 6 is linked to the cognitive dissonance theory (Festinger, 1957, 1964), where the basic premise is that an individual strives for consistency or consonance among his or her cognition, thus affecting the tacit dimension.

Framing the situation

The purpose of the framing process is here understood as the clarification of the value basis on the part of the organisation members, in addition to the clarification of the relevance the situation has for the latter.

The framing process can to a considerable extent be compared with Goffman's (1959) idea that it is critical to understand what sort of situation we are in and how we are expected to behave in this situation. In this way framing the situation will be closely linked to problem definition and to Schutz' (1990 Vol.: 1-3) understanding of how actors in a situation define the social world. Schutz and Goffman's point is that we present different aspects of ourselves to others. It is in other words only with a part of ourselves that we enter social contexts. Schutz underlines the importance of relevance relative to the interests at stake in the concrete situation. It is relevance and the person's conviction which constitute the most important elements when a person frames a situation. What Schutz wants to emphasise is the fact that an infinite number of social realities can appear for a person, if he does not frame the situation and decide on the status it has for him. It is furthermore the importance we attach to our experiences which will constitute the framework of the situation we enter, i.e. the emphasise we give the tacit dimension (Polanyi, 1966).

One thing is how we introduce ourselves in a situation, another is how we assess others when they introduce themselves in the same situation. The point is that the social world is constructed by us through our knowledge at hand. Thus a circular process will be in operation. I.e.: It is not so that we receive impressions, signals, symbols and information etc. from the other(s), and then interpret the impressions. It is just as much a process the other way. We construct some notions and then look for signs, symbols, information etc., with which these actions are in harmony in relation to the other party. In this way we manage to sustain our cognitive pattern and prejudice without new information dramatically budging our previous experience. Understood in this way the construction of a social reality is a conservative process for each and every one of us, and has an inhibiting effect on our ability to frame the situation in a way conducive to innovation processes, i.e. the opening of the cognitive loop.

The learning loop and tacit knowledge

Tacit knowledge can be a key barrier to innovation, e.g. when the organisation introduce a new production method or when a new product is being developed. This is because tacit knowledge usually is part of a long term learning process in a specific context, being embodied in the structure of thinking, the way of thinking, and therefor functions as a conservative element in relation to innovation. But on the other hand, tacit knowledge is a sort of organisational ´imune´ system hindering imitation from other social systems, and promoting continuos improvement. The function of tacit knowledge is then both conservative, i.e. stabilising the system, and acting as an imitation ´guard´. The propositions (proposition 7 and 7a) are then that tacit knowledge promotes continuos improvement but hinders innovation within an organisation, depending on the turbulence and competition in the market, and hinders imitation from competitors. There are some balancing arguments to these propositions, which are shown in fig. 5, and discussed below in connection with fig. 6..

Proposition 7: Tacit knowledge sustains our cognitive pattern and hinder continuos innovation processes, but promote continuos improvement in the system.

Proposition 7a: Tacit knowledge function as an organisational imune-system, hindering imitation from other social systems.

Fig. 2 Tacit knowledge-innovation and imitation

Turbulence and competition in the market

	Little	High
High complexity in the work-process	Tacit knowledge promotes continuos improvement and continuos innovation but hinder imitation	Tacit knowledge promotes continuos improvement but hinder continuos innovation and imitation
Low	Tacit knowledge promotes continuos improvement and continuos innovation but does not hinder imitation	Tacit knowledge promotes continuos improvement, and hinders continuos innovation, but does not hinder imitation

Tacit knowledge is the practical knowledge used to perform a task, and it is also «the knowledge that is used as a tool to handle what is being focused on» (Sveiby, 1997: 30). Consequently, tacit knowledge is in the business context: practical, action oriented, experience-based, context- linked and personal, but not subjective or relative. It is objective, i.e. can be tested, checked, investigated empirically, in the sense that it is objective in its consequences. This means that the work done by using tacit knowledge can be tested for quality, durability, and reductions in the cost of production. Tacit knowledge is as real as explicit knowledge, but the processes to acquire this kind of knowledge, i.e. tacit knowing, rely on awareness of details which cannot be specified or tested in any known scientific way. But this does not apply to tacit knowledge, which is the outcome of the processes of tacit knowing. Tacit knowing is a process of a complex whole, a pattern which escapes when taken apart for analysis. But tacit knowing is not only involved in the process by which tacit knowledge is gained. It is also involved in the processes by which all knowledge is gained (Polanyi, 1958: 49-69). For Polanyi (1958) tacit knowing is the dominant principle of all knowledge.

We are now trying to bring the typology in fig. 2 into a conceptual model integrating both the normative closed loop and the cognitively open loop, to a more practical level, anyhow, it is our purpose with the conceptual model shown in fig. 3

Fig. 3 Tacit knowledge, continuos improvement, continuos innovation and new technology

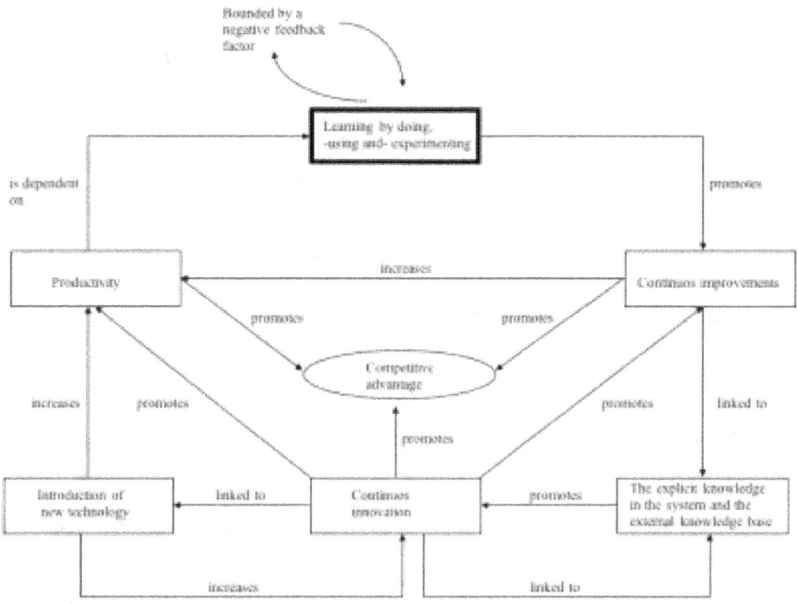

Learning by- doing,- using and- experimenting is here seen as the processes constituting tacit knowledge. Tacit knowledge is bounded by a negative feedback factor, thus tacit knowledge promotes continuos improvement only to a certain level, and then declines. Solow (1997: 25) denotes this phenomenon as «bounded learning by doing». We, however, go a step further and assume that all tacit knowledge has this effect on continuos improvement. When continuos improvement is linked to the explicit knowledge in the system, and the systems external knowledge base (via the learning loop in fig. 1), continuos innovation appears in irregular streams, increasing productivity and promoting competitive advantage. Continuos improvement may also increase productivity, but is also here bounded by the negative feedback factor. This is in line with Solow (1997: 24) who argues:»The routine continuos improvement of products and processes is arguably the most important source of increased productivity in mature industries», i.e. the experience based part of the firms knowledge base. Continuos improvement may also promote competitive advantage directly by e.g. increasing the quality of the product.

The external knowledge base is an endogenous element in the model, and is linked to the cognitively open loop and the learning loop. Our working assumption here is thus that continuos improvement, not continuos innovation, is what tacit knowledge is actually about. However linked to the external knowledge base, something new may occur and innovation is brought into the system. Both continuos improvement and continuos innovations is created by the interaction between the normative closed loop, the cognitively open loop and the learning loop. That continuos innovations promote continuos improvement is shown by Fruin (1997) at Toshiba. Continuos innovations may be understood as punctuation's of continuos improvements (Fruin, 1997:27).

When no innovation occurs in the model, continuos improvement increases productivity, but only to a certain degree. When at a certain time innovation enters the model productivity will increase to a higher level, which gives a positive bandwagon effect upon learning by- doing,- using and- experimenting, because something new brings the learning process to a higher level of achievement. Innovation and new technology opens up a new field for learning, which give learning by- doing,- using and -experimenting a new input factor, even if the bounded negative feedback factor still is in operation, i.e. it is in operation, but at a new level of achievement.

Learning by- doing,- using and- experimenting is here seen as generalised tacit knowledge. The more this generalised tacit knowledge is conservative, i.e. not linked effectively to the cognitive open loop, the more it is bounded by the negative feedback factor, and vice versa.

Imitation is part of continuos improvement and continuos innovation, but only to a certain degree, because tacit knowledge is difficult to imitate. Tacit knowledge then function as a guard for imitation (Attewell, 1992), thus at a global level function as a conservative factor hindering continuos improvements and continuos innovations to diffuse between systems.

The introduction of new technology will increase continuos

innovation, because new possibilities enter the ground floor realities and creative leaps may penetrate and change the ways old «facts» are understood, introducing new patterns of understanding. Solow (1997: 32) says:» ---the trend of productivity depends in a complex way on the timing of successive innovations and on the pace of investment during the random intervals within which a particular generation of technology is at the frontier». But, it is continuos improvement based on the generalised tacit knowledge in the firm, which can bring productivity up to a higher ratio compared to competitors, because it can't be bought in the market; it has to be developed inside the firm, as a general rule. Thus tacit knowledge has three faces: one conservative, bounding the improvement process. A second one is guarding the firm from imitations, and a third one is giving the little bit extra to the productivity process.

The greater the intensity in the process of learning by-doing,- using and-experimenting, the greater will the productivity gain from the processes in the whole model. Thus, tacit knowledge plays the central role in the productivity of firms, both in steady state situations, but even more in a hypercompetitive marked (Dáveni, 1994).

Since continuos improvements, continuos innovations and the implementation of new technologies happens at different rates, i.e. they are connected nonlinearly, the turbulent situation is not only in the hypercompetitive marked, but also inside the firm. To damper the internal turbulence the conservative element of tacit knowledge is in operation.

When it comes to learning by experimenting, Fruin (1997:14) says: «Factory-based experimentation with and refinement of routines, skill sets, and practices are among the most useful successful things learned». This is an organizational form where tacit knowledge is linked to the explicit knowledge base in the firm and the external knowledge base. The point here is however, as with all innovations that the value added (Va) is relatively higher than the cost (c) of learning by- experimenting, using, and -doing, and the same argument goes for introduction of new technology, i.e. innovations should always be related to the following relation:

Va > C

The rate of productivity is limited by the rate of technological progress, continuos innovation and continuos improvements. Continuos improvement, however is linked to the stock of human capital, i.e. knowledge, and :»The accumulation of human capital appears to be much more a matter of quality than of quantity» (Solow, 1997: 77). And this brings us to the real contribution of the model (fig. 6): To turn theoretical and practical attention to tacit knowledge, here: learning by-doing,- using and- experimenting, i.e. the interwoven experiences of the people at work, using their knowledge at hand, reflecting upon it, and learning from this process, to the benefit of the firm, the wider environment, and the future.

Conclusion

The social autopoietical system is a normatively closed and cognitively open system. In order to describe, explain and predict stability and innovation in social systems by means of the autopoiesis theory, we have in this chapter used an analytical model where the following constructs have been in focus: The normative super-structure, the normatively closed loop, the cognitively open loop, the learning loop and the field-protection loop. In addition we have made use of the constructs model-weak and model-strong actors and systems. It is the relationship between all these constructs we consider to be useful in order to describe, explain and predict stability and innovation in organisations regarded as social systems by means of the autopoiesis theory.

An organisation has a need for finding the proper balance between internal and external learning. The theory also gives direction for knowledge creation, knowledge integration and the practical use of knowledge, i.e. a knowledge theory of the firm. In the theory, this is done without focusing at the hierarchy as a co-ordinating mechanism. It is the cognitive open structures which make up the necessary condition for co-ordination, and at the same time the normative closed modus of the system integrates the knowledge. Rules and directives, which constitutes the traditional, bureaucratic model for integration and co-ordination of knowledge, is transformed with the coexistence of the normatively closed loop and cognitively open loop. In this theory it is information and knowledge from the actors in the activity systems, i.e. what the systems is designed to do, which is in focus, not rules and directives in a bureaucratic hierarchy focused on power-structures and positions.

A simplified presentation of the chapter's contents aimed at bringing the main message across regarding the innovation potential for organisations from an autopoietical perspective as used by us, is seen in fig. 4.

Insert Figure 4 Social autopoiesis and organizational innovation

	Power systems (Internaly acting. Little innovation potential)	Learning systems (Acting externally. Great innovation potential)
Model strong systems		
Model weak systems	Crisis systems (Procedure and rule oriented. Very little innovation potential)	Epigone systems (Externally seeking. Moderate innovation potential)
	Cognitively closed systems (Few system-environment relations)	Cognitively open systems (Many system-environment relations)

The main message in figure 4 is that explicit models and cognitively open systems are conducive to learning and have a great innovation potential, depending on the tacit dimension which could function as a conservative element. A practical implication is that those who have model power must clarify and make visible the normative basis, i.e. their own models, in addition to the models the system is intended to use.

In order to make the processes which are operational in changes of autopoietical systems visible, we have used the following constructs:

The system-specific normative basis, selection processes, expectations, experiences, communication, problem definition, and framing the situation. It is the mechanisms in these processes in addition to the relationship between them we have analysed in this chapter.

Our emphasis in this chapter has been on the fact that the normative basis must be made explicit if the system is to show potential for continuos innovation. Methodologically this could happen through the following phases:

Phase I: Reflection over one's own epistemology and the normative basis of the system. Examples of questions from this initial phase could be:

a) What are our basic assumptions?

b) What implications do these assumptions have for our behaviour?

c) What is our value system?

d) What implications does our value system have for our behaviour?

e) What is the normative basis of the system?

f) What implications does this have for our behaviour?

g) What is the normative basis for the super-structure?

h) What implications does this have for our behaviour?

i) What models do we use in our daily work as a result of a-h?

j) What makes these models explicit?.

Phase II

Define the problems confronting the system on the basis of the models made visible in the two final points in phase I (i and j).

A methodology for autopoietical systems to be deduced from the previous description, is the following:

A. Introduce a routine where the actors must reflect on the normative basis of the system and the normative superstructure. In practice a person not belonging to the concrete field should be brought in, in order to initiate the self-reflection process.

B. Introduce a routine which consciously changes perspective in a meeting context in order to spotlight more aspects of the problem/phenomenon to be questioned. In practice a person who does not belong to the concrete field should be brought in, in order to initiate and continue the process.

Based upon the arguments in this chapter we propose aspects of a theory of organizational innovation based on social autopoiesis theory in fig. 5.

Fig. 5 Organizational innovation processes based on social autopoiesis theory

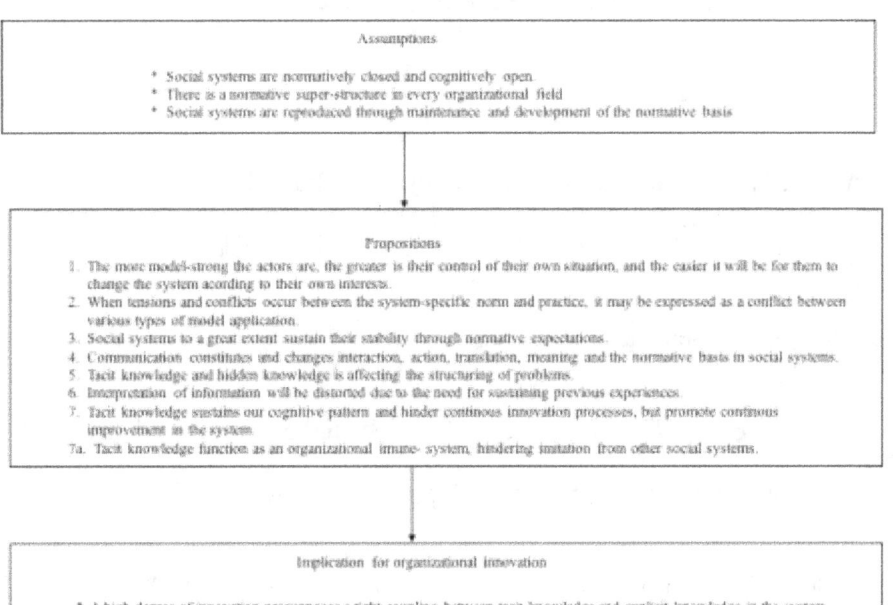

References

Ashby, W.R. (1961). An Introduction to Cybernetics, Chapman & Hall LTD, New York.

Ashby, W.R. (1968). Principles of the Self-Organizing System. In W. Buckley (Ed.). Modern Systems Research for the Behavioral Scientist, pp.: 108-123, Aldine, Chicago, Ill.

Ashby, W.R.(1970)"Connectance of Large Dynamic (Cybernetic) Systems: Critical Values for Stability", Nature, Vol 228 no. 5273 Nov. 21, 1970.

Ashby, W.R. (1981)"Constraint Analysis of Many Dimensional Relations", In Conant, R. (Ed.) "Mechanisms of Intelligence", Intersystems Seaside, California.

Attewell, P. (1992). Technology diffusion and organizational learning: The case of business computing, Organizational Science, 3, 1: 1-19.

Bandler, R. & Grinder, J. (1975). The Structure of Magia. Vol I and II, Science and Behavior Books, Palo Alto, Cal.

Bateson, G. (1972). Steps to an Ecology of Mind. Intex Books, London.

Bateson, G. (1988). Mind and Nature, (Swedish Translation, 1988, Symposium & Tryckeri, Stockholm.)

Borei, J.M. (1992). Chaos to community: One company's journey towards transformation, World Business Academy Perspectives, 6,2: 67-79.

Bourdieu, P. (1984). Distinction: A Social Critique of the Judgement of Taste, Routledge & Kegan Paul, London.

Bourdieu, P. (1988). Homo Academicus, Polity Press, Cambridge.

Bourdieu, P. (1992). An invitation to reflective sociology, Polity Press, New York.

Broady, D. (1991). Sociologi och Epistemologi: Om Pierre Bourdieus författerskap och den historiska epistemologin, HLS Førlag, Stockholm.

Bråten, S. (1973). Model Monopoly and Communication. Acta Sociologica, 16, 2: 98-107.

Bråten, S. (1984). The Third Position: Beyond artificial and autopoietic reduction, Kybernetes, 13: 157-163.

Bråten, S. (1986). The Third Position: Beyond Artificial and

Autopoietic Reduction. In Geyer, F. & J. Van der Zouwen (eds.). Sociocybernetic Paradoxes,: 193-205, Sage, Beverly Hills.

Bunge, M.(1983). Exploring the World. Dordrecht: Reidel.

Bunge, M.(1983a). Understanding the World. Dordrecht: Reidel.

Bunge, M. (1985). Philosophy of Science and Technology. Part I. Dordrecht: Reidel.

Bunge, M. (1985a). Philosophy of Science and Technology. Part II. Dordrecht: Reidel.

Bunge, M. (1989). Ethics: The Good and the Right, Reidel, Dordrecht.

Bunge, M. (1992). Systems Everywhere, In Negoita, C.V. (ed.), Cybernetics and Applied Systems,pp. 23-43, Marcell Deker, New York.

Bunge, M. (1996). Finding philosophy in social science, Yale University Press, London.

Bunge, M. (1997). Mechanism and explanation, Philosophy of the Social Sciences, 27, 4:410-465.

DÁveni, R. (1994). Hypercompetition: Managing the dynamics of strategic maneuvering, The Free Press, New York.

Festinger, L. (1957). A theory of cognitive dissonance. Stanford

University Press, Stanford, CA.

Festinger, L. (1964). Conflict, decision and dissonance. Stanford University Press, Stanford, CA.

Fishbein, M. & Ajzen, I. (1975). Belief, attitude, intention and behavior: An introduction to theory and research, Addison-Wesley, Reading, M.A.

Foerster, H.V. (1981). Observing Systems, Intersystems Publications, Seaside, Cal.

Fruin, W.M. (1997). Knowledge Works: Managing intellectual capital at Toshiba, Oxford University Press Oxford.

Geyer, R.F. & J. Van der Zouwen (eds.). (1978). Sociocybernetics: An Actor-Oriented Social Systems Approach, Vol. 1 & 2, Martinus Nijhoff, Leiden.

Geyer, R.F. & Van der Zouwen (1992). Sociocybernetics. In Negoita, C.V. Cybernetics and Applied Systems,: 95-124, Marcel Dekker, New York.

Goffman, E. (1959). Presentation of Self in Everyday Life, Anchor Books, New York.

Johannessen, J-A. (1994). Cybernetics and Innovation: The `Hopeless`Choice between Stability and Innovation" Entrepreneurship

Innovation and Change, 2,3: 249-263.

Johannessen, J-A. (1995). Basic Features of an Information and Communication System Aimed at Promoting Organizational Learning, Systems Practice, Vol. 8, No. 2: 183-197.

Johannessen, J-A. (1996). Systemics applied to the study of organizational fields: developing a research strategy, Kybernetes, 25, 1: 33-51.

Johannessen, J-A. (1997). Aspects of ethics in systemic thinking, Kybernetes (Forthcomming, Vol. 26).

Johannessen, J-A. & Hauan, A. (1994). Communication. A System Theoretical Point of View, Systems Practice, 7, nr. 1:63-73.

Judge, W.Q., Fryxell, G.E. & Dooley, R.S. (1997). The new task of R&D management: Creating goal directed communities for innovation, California Management Review, 39, 3: 72-85.

Kelley, H.H. (1950). The warm-cold variable in first impressions of persons. Journal of Personality, 18: 431-439.

Luhmann, N. (1975). Soziologische Aufklärung, Vol. 1-5, Westdeutscher Verlag, Berlin.

Luhmann, N. (1982). The World Society as a Social System.

International Journal of General Systems, 8: 131-138.

Luhmann, N. (1986). The autopoiesis of social systems. In F. Geyer and J. van der Zouwen (eds,). Sociocybernetic Paradoxes. Sage. Beverly Hills, CA. pp. 172-192.

Luhmann, N. (1990). Essays on Self reference, Columbia University Press, New York.

Luhmann, N. (1992). Ecological Communication. Polity Press. Cambridge.

Luhmann, N. (1995). Lykke og ulykke, kommunikasjon inden for familier: Om patologiens genese, In J.C. Jacobsen (ed.). Autopoiesis, Vol. II, Politisk Revy, København.

Maturana, H. (1981). Autopoiesis, in Zeleny, M. (Ed.). Autopoiesis: A Theory of Living Organization, Elsevier, New York, pp. 21-23.

Maturana, H.R. & Varela, F.J. (1980). Autopoiesis and cognition: The realization of the living, Reidel, Dordrecht.

Maturana, H.R. & Varela, F.J. (1987). The tree of Knowledge, New Science Library, London.

McGuire, W.J. (1985). Attitudes and attitude change. I. G. Lindzey & E. Aronson (red.), Handbook of sosial psychology, Vol. 2 (233-346),

Random House, New York.

Merton, R.K. (1968). Social Theory and Social Structure, Free Press, New York.

Mingers, J. (1989). An Introduction to Autopoiesis: Implications and Applications. Systems Practice, 2: 159-180.

Myrdal, G. (1944). An American Dilemma: The Negro Problem and Modern Democracy, Harper, New York.

Parsons, T. (1967). Sociological Theory and Modern Society, Free Press, New York.

Peck, M.S. (1985). The different drum, Simon & Schuster, New York.

Polanyi, M. (1958). Personal Knowledge: Towards a post-critical philosophy, The University Chicago Press, Chicago.

Polanyi, M. (1962). Knowledge and Being, Routledge, New York.

Polanyi, M. (1966). The tacit dimension, Doubleday, Garden City, NJ.

Popovic, D. (1992). Foreword. In Negoita, C.V. (ed.). Cybernetics and Applied Systems, Marcel Dekker, New York.

Robb, F. (1989). Cybernetics and Supra Human Autopoetic Systems.

Systems Practice, 2: 47-74.

Robb, F. (1989a). The Application of Autopoietic Systems to Social Organizations: A Comment on John Mingers: An Introduction to Autopoiesis: Implications and Applications. Systems Practice, 2: 349-351.

Robb, F. (1992). Are institutions Entities of a Natural Kind? A Consideration of the Outlook of Mankind. In Negoita (Eds.). Cybernetics and Applied Systems,: 149-163, Marcel Dekker, New York.

Rød Larsen, T. (1976). Hjerte og hjerne, Stensilskrifter fra institutt for Rettssosiologi, University of Oslo Press, Oslo.

Schutz, A. (1990). The Problem of Social Reality. Collected Chapters, Vol. 1, 2 and 3. Kluwer Academic Publishers, London.

Senge, P. (1990). The leaders new work: Building learning organizations, Sloan Management Review, 32,1: 7-23.

Sheppard, B.H., Hartwick, J. & Warshaw, P.R. (1988). The Theory of Reasoned Action: A meta-Analysis of Past Research With Recommendations for Modifications and Future Research. Journal of Consumer Research, 15: 325-343.

Solow, R.M. (1997). Learning from learning by doing: Lessons for economic growth, Stanford University Press, Stanford, California.

Sveiby, K.E. (1997). The new organizational wealth: managing & measuring knowledge- based assets, Berrett-Koehler, San Francisco.

Ulrich, W. (1983). Critical Heuristics of Social Planning: A New Approach to Practical Philosophy, Haupl, Bern.

Ulrich, W. (1986). Critical Heuristics of Social System Design, Working Chapter 10, Department of Management Systems and Sciences, University of Hull.

Ulrich, W. (1987). Critical Heuristics of Social Systems Design, European Journal of Operational Research, 31: 276-283.

Ulrich, W. (1988). System Thinking, Systems Practice, and Practical Philosophy: A Program for Research, Systems Practice, 1: 137-163.

Varela, F.G. (1979). Principles of Biological Autonomy, Elsevier, New York.

Von Bertalanffy, L. (1973). General Systems Theory, Harmondsworth, New York.

Watzlawick,P. (1984). Self-Fulfilling Prophecies, In P. Watzlawick (Ed.). The Invented Reality, W.W. Norton & Company, London.

Wiener, N. (1947). Cybernetics: or Control and Communication in the Animal and the Machine, MIT Press, Cambridge, Mass.

Chapter on concepts

Ambidextrous organizations. *Ambidextrous organizations* are organizations that have the ability to adapt to changes in external conditions while at the same time generating their own future by means of, among other things, performance improvement, growth and innovation (Duncan, 1976; O'Reilly & Tushman, 2004, 2006, 2011; Thota & Munir, 2011). In chapter 6, we have shown how ambidextrous organizations can be developed by HR departments.

In 2004, O'Reilly & Tushman expressed that ambidextrous organizations would constitute one of the major challenges for management in the global knowledge economy.

The findings of O'Reilly & Tushman (2004) were overwhelming. Regarding the launching of radical innovations, they found that none of the cross-functional or unsupported teams and only a quarter of the teams with functional designs were able to produce radical innovations. However, among the ambidextrous organizations, 90% were successful in producing radical innovations. Empirical research has shown that this type of organizational design is best for producing both incremental and radical innovations (Thora & Munir, 2011).

Asplund's motivation theory[5]. In brief, this theory can be described in the following way: *People are motivated by social responses* (Asplund, 2010: 221-229). The following statement may be said to be a central point made by Asplund's theory: *When people receive social responses, their level of activity increases.*

Asplund's motivation theory is consistent with North's action theory (ref. North's action theory). Understood in this way, it seems reasonable to connect the two theories in the statement: *People are motivated by the social responses rewarded by the institutional framework.*

Availability cascades. This refers to the idea that we are all controlled

---

[5] Asplund's motivation theory, a term we use here, is based on Asplund's research..

by the image of reality created by the media, because this image is easy to retrieve from memory.

Availability proposition. This may be expressed as follow: The more easily information enters into our consciousness, the greater the likelihood that we will have confidence in that information. In other words, we believe more in the type of information that is available in memory than the information that is not so readily available.

Behavioural perspective. This perspective focuses on the behaviour of employees as an explanation for the relationship between business strategy and the results obtained.

Boudon-Coleman diagram. This research methodology was developed by Mario Bunge (Bunge, 1978:76-79) based on insights made by the sociologists Boudon and Coleman. The purpose of the diagram is to show the relationship between the various levels, such as the macro and micro-levels. For instance, it is shown how changes at the macro-level, such as technological innovations in feudal society, can lead to increased income at the micro-level. However, it was shown that technological innovations could lead to weakening of the semi-feudal structures because dependency on land owners was reduced. Consequently, the landowners opposed such changes especially in the case of technological innovations, which Boudon has shown in his research (Boudon, 1981: 100). Coleman (Coleman, 1990: 7-12) started at the macro level, went to the individual level to find explanations and finally ended up at the macro level again.

An important purpose of Bunge's Boudon-Coleman diagram is to identify social mechanisms that maintain or change the phenomenon or problem under investigation (as mentioned above, in Boudon's analysis of semi-feudal society). Bunge's Boudon-Coleman diagram may be said to represent a "mixed strategy"; Bunge says the following: *When studying systems of any kind a) reduce them to their components (at some level) and the interaction among these, as well as among them and environmental items, but acknowledge and explain emergence* (see the chapter on concepts) *whenever it occurs, and b) approach systems from all pertinent sides and on all relevant levels, integrating theories or even research fields whenever unidisciplinarity proves to be insufficient* (Bunge, 1998:78). The purpose of this research strategy is to arrive at a deeper and more complete explanation of a system's behaviour.

Capabilities. Capabilities are for an organization what abilities are for an individual.

An organizational capability may thus be defined as an organization's ability to perform a task, activity or process. Operational capabilities enable an organization to make money in the here and now (Winter, 2003: 991-995). Dynamic capabilities, as opposed to operational capabilities, are linked to processes of change. Change and innovation are at the centre of dynamic capabilities.

Simplified, one may say that organizational capabilities are something an organization does well compared to its competitors (Ulrich and Brockbank, 2005). These capabilities are intangible and therefore difficult for competitors to imitate (Wernerfelt, 1984).

Cohesive energy. In a social system cohesive energy is "the glue" that binds the system together. Cohesive energy is the social mechanisms that make the system durable. According to systemic thinking it is the relationships and actions that bind social systems together. The rationale is that relationships and the systems of relationships may be said to control human behaviour. Social systems are held together (in systemic thinking) by dynamic social relations (e.g. feelings, perceptions, norms) and social action (e.g. cooperation, solidarity, conflict and communication).

Co-creation. Co-creation involves working together to promote knowledge processes and innovation. If knowledge processes and innovation are essential for value creation in the knowledge society, co-creation is an important social mechanism for initiating, maintaining and strengthening these processes. The balance between competition and cooperation, embodied in the concept of co-creation, leads to constructive criticism and the necessary scope of knowledge that exists in the network so as to promote creativity and the innovative. Instead of a zero-sum situation, a positive-sum situation will be developed where everyone wins.

Collective blindness. Collective blindness may be said to be a form of collective arrogance, which results in irrational actions. Minor events slip under the radar, causing the system to not be fully aware of what is happening. Politicians' explanations why voters in a referendum vote contrary to what most of the power elite and the media advocated is an example of collective blindness.

Competence. Competence refers to knowledge, skills and attitudes.

Core Competence. The concept was popular in the strategy literature of the 1990s. Core competence may be defined as: *"a bundle of skills and technologies that enable a company to provide a particular benefit to customers"* (Hamel & Prahalad, 1996:219). More recently, core competence as a concept has been given less attention in the research on dynamic capabilities, and now there is more focus on the concept of *fitness*. The term *evolutionary fitness* is also used in the research literature in connection with technology, quality, cost development, market development, innovation and competitive positioning (Helfat, et al, 2007: 7).

Discontinuous innovations. These are innovations that change the premises of technology, markets, our mindset, and so on. We know that sooner or later discontinuous innovations will emerge in the future (Hewing, 2013).

Dynamic capabilities. Dynamic capabilities stem from the resource-based perspective and evolutionary thinking in strategy literature (Teece, 2013: 3-65; 82-113; Nelson and Winter, 1982). The dynamic perspective attempts to explain what promotes an organization's competitive position over time through innovation and growth (Teece, 2013: x).

The original thinking concerning dynamic capabilities may be related to Teece et al. (1997). These authors defined dynamic capabilities as *an organization's ability to create, develop and modify its internal and external expertise in order to address changes in the external world.*

Dynamic capabilities are now seen as all the organizational processes, not only internal and external expertise, that contribute to an organization's capacity to adapt to change while creating the organization's future.

Explicit knowledge. This is knowledge that can be digitized and communicated to others as information.

Evidence. This may be results, such as research results, that can be relied on. However, it is also important to be aware of the fact that other evidence may be available without having to refer to figures and quantities, such as evidence that emerges from observations and good judgment without the assessment being quantified. Evidence-based research is research results that are based on approved and accepted scientific research methods.

Emergent. An emergent occurs if something new turns up on one level that has not previously existed on the level below. With emergent we mean: *Let S be a system with composition A, i.e. the various components in addition to the way they are composed. If P is a property of S, P is emergent with regard to A, if and only if no components in A possess P; otherwise P is to be regarded as a resulting property with regards to A.* (Bunge, 1977:97).

Entrepreneurial spirit. The entrepreneurial spirit may be described as follows (Roddick, 2003: 106-107):

- The vision of something new and belief in this that is so strong that belief becomes reality.
- A touch of positive madness.
- The ability to stand out from the crowd.

- Creative tension bubbling over.
- Pathological optimism.
- To act before you know!
- Basic desire for change.
- Creative energy focused on ideas, not on explicit factual knowledge.
- Being able to tell the story you want to sell.

Feedback Giving the other person feedback, for instance with regard to their behaviour, attitudes, and the like, is the most important element in the area of interactive skills and emotional intelligence (Goleman, 1996; 2007). Analysis of feedback is a sure way to identify our strengths and then reinforce them (Wang, et al., 2003). Failure to give people feedback on their behavior in some contexts may even be considered immoral.

Feed-forward. Feed-forward is regarded here as an expectation mechanism. It seems reasonable to assume that our expectations influence our behaviour in the present. It is therefore important that we make explicit to ourselves the expectations we have of a situation. By making expectations explicit, we have a greater opportunity to learn from our experiences and thus improve our performance.

Front line focus. This refers to those in the front line, i.e. in direct contact with customers, users, patients, students, etc. They have the greatest expertise, necessary information, and decision-making authority and are regarded as the most important resource in the organization because they are at the point where an organization's value creation occurs.

Global competence network. These competence networks may be divided into political, social, economic, technological and cultural patterns. It is when these five patterns interact that one may perceive the overall pattern. In the global knowledge economy it seems reasonable to assume that those who control this pattern set the conditions for economic development. These global competence networks will most likely make an impact on HR departments in companies competing for this kind of expertise in national markets.

Global competence networks are also emphasized as crucial for economic growth by OECD (2001), although they use the term *innovative clusters.* The purpose of innovative clusters and global competence networks is the development, dissemination and use of new ideas that promote wealth creation.

There is much to suggest that a greater degree of integration and cooperation between private and public sectors at the national and regional levels is an important prerequisite for initiating the innovative locomotive effect. The global competence networks are metaphorically the energy source that sustains the motion of this locomotive. It would be counterproductive to replace the locomotive once in motion. Conversely, the individual carriages of the locomotive (read: organizational level) can be changed depending on their competitive position. The individual passengers on the train create ideas and knowledge through the processes that may be called *creative chaos*. In this way we will arrive at a tripartite of the prerequisites for global competence networks. At the individual level, creative chaos occurs. At the organizational level, there will be creative destruction. At the social and global levels, creative collaboration takes place. These three processes create innovation and economic growth as an emergent, not as a *future perfectum,* i.e. a planned process with given results.

A prerequisite for the reasoning above is that tension and competition at one level requires collaboration at another level. Competition and cooperation are both necessary if one is to develop innovation and economic growth, in the same manner that stability and change are necessary for flexibility. Too much of the one (stability) leads to rigidity, and too much of the other (change) leads to chaos. Understood in this way, emergents cannot be planned.

Hamel's Law of Innovation. The "law" states that only between one and two of one thousand ideas become innovations in a market (Hamel, 2002; 2012). Therefore, an infostructure must be created to ensure that ideas are continuously produced in a business.

Hidden knowledge. Hidden knowledge is what we do not know we do not know. Kirzner (1982) says that hidden knowledge is possibly the most important knowledge domain of creativity, innovation and entrepreneurship.

History's "slow fields".

This refers to the fact that norms, values and actions tend to be in operation long after the functions, activities and processes that initially created them disappear, thus generating so-called *slow fields of history*. These norms, values and actions exist though they have no apparent function, contributing to maintaining a type of behaviour long after the type of behaviour is functional or meaningful[6]. For sociologists and historians it is important to determine whether norms and values have any function, or whether they are part of history's slow fields. By examining history's slow fields, it may be possible to provide better explanations for phenomena.

HR management. HR management is defined as HR practices at various levels (micro, meso, macro) for managing people in organizations.

HR management has been defined in many different ways. For instance, Boxall and Purcell (2003:1) define HR management as all those activities oriented towards managing relations between employees in an organization. This definition emphasizes the relational perspective. Later, they expanded their definition to include all the activities and processes that underpin an organization's value creation (Boxall and Purcell,

---

[6] Asplund (1970: 55) refers to a similar phenomenon when he discusses Simmel. He points out that the norms that may have had a positive function during a historic phase become in a later phase dysfunctional.

2010:29). On this basis, Armstrong defines the activities and processes that HR management should engage in: *"HRM covers activities such as human capital management, knowledge management, organizational design and development, resource planning (recruitment, talent development), performance management, organizational learning, reward systems, relationships between employees, and employees' wellness."* (Armstrong, 2014:6). However, we believe Armstrong underestimates two essential areas of knowledge in his definition: the management of innovation processes, and change processes in organizations. Innovation and change are strongly emphasized in the global HRM Survey (White & Younger, 2013:35-39). Armstrong has included the ethical perspective in his Handbook for HRM (Armstrong, 2014a:95-105). Management of innovation processes and change processes in organizations is also highlighted and underlined by Wright et al. (2011: 5) in their description of HRM. However, it must also be said that Armstrong discusses innovation (Armstrong, 2014:145-155), but not in his process definition of HR management. Innovation and change processes are also emphasized by Ulrich et al. (2013). Brockbank (2013: 24) especially mentions these two processes as being important in the research model Ulrich et al. (2013) have developed through their empirical research over 25 years.

Implicit Knowledge. This is knowledge that is spread throughout an organization but not integrated.

Information input overload. This occurs when an individual, a team, an organization or a community receive more information than they can manage to process.

In a situation characterised by information input overload the following may occur (Miller, 1978: 123):

1. Designated tasks and responsibilities are left undone
2. Errors are made
3. Queues of information occur
4. Information is filtered out that should have been included
5. Abstract formulations are made when they should have been specific
6. Communication channels are overloaded, creating stress and tension in the system
7. Complex situations are shunned
8. Information is lumped together for processing

Each of the above eight points may result in a decrease in efficiency when the system is exposed to information input overload.

Infostructure. The infostructure concerns the processes that enable the development, transfer, analysis, storage, coordination and management of data, information and knowledge. The infostructure consists of eleven generic processes, as shown in Fig. 8 in this book. The eleven processes in the infostructure may be considered as nodes in a social network at different levels, for example team, organization, society, and region, all in the global space. Together, the eleven processes comprise the totality of the infostructure.

It may be said that the *info*structure has the same importance in the knowledge society as the *infra*structure had in the industrial society.

Innovation. Innovation is here understood as any idea, practice or material element, which is perceived as new for the person using it (Zaltman et al., 1973).

Ideas are seen as the smallest unit in the innovation process (Hamel, 2002; 2012). However, this refers to the ideas that are in process of development and not fully developed ideas. Before an idea can be characterized as innovative, it must prove to be beneficial to somebody, i.e. the market must accept the idea and apply it. Consequently, the creative process of innovation is here understood as the benefit it has for a market (Amabile, 1990; Johannessen, et al., 2001: 25). Thus, it is not sufficient that an idea is new for it to be considered an innovation. An idea may have a great degree of novelty, but if it is of no benefit to anybody in the market, then it has no innovative value.

Kaizen. This is a Japanese method, which means that an organization develops systems for organized improvement (Maurer, 2012).

Knowledge. The definition of knowledge used here is *the systematization and structuring of information for one or more goals or purposes.*

Knowledge worker. A knowledge worker has been described by the OECD as *a person whose primary task is to generate and apply knowledge*, rather than to provide services or produce physical products

(OECD, 2000 a, b, c, d, e; 2001). This may be understood as a *formal definition* of a knowledge worker.

This definition does not restrict knowledge workers to creative fields, as is the case with, for example, Mosco and McKercher (2007: vii–xxiv). The OECD definition also allows for the fact that a knowledge worker may perform routine tasks. The definition also does not limit the type of work performed by knowledge workers to tasks relating to creative problem-solving strategies, unlike the definition provided by Reinhardt et al. (2011).

Knowledge enterprise. This is an enterprise that has knowledge as its most significant output. It is perhaps helpful to think of the process *input - process - output* to separate industrial enterprises from knowledge enterprises. Much knowledge and skills are needed to produce high-tech products such as computers, and there are also many knowledge workers involved in this process. However, the majority of products produced today are high-tech industrial products, and although such products require very skilled knowledge in the production process, they are nevertheless output-industrial products.

On the other hand, law firms, consulting firms and universities are examples of knowledge enterprises.

Knowledge management. Management of knowledge resources in an organization. These resources may be explicit knowledge, implicit knowledge, tacit knowledge and hidden knowledge.

Locomotive effect. This refers to something that generates and then reinforces an activity or development.

Modularization. An extreme fragmentation of the production process in the global knowledge economy. Production is fragmented and distributed according to the following logic: Costs – quality – competence – design – innovation.

Modular flexibility. The modulization of value creation. Modular flexibility may best be understood as the globalization of production processes, and extreme specialization of work processes with a focus on core processes.

Necessary and sufficient conditions. It may often be appropriate to divide conditions or premises into *necessary conditions* and *sufficient conditions*. Necessary conditions must be present to trigger an action, but these may not be sufficient. The sufficient conditions must also be present to trigger the action.

North's action theory[7]. This action theory may be expressed in the following statement: *People act on the basis of a system of rewards as expressed in the norms, values, rules and attitudes in the culture (the institutional framework)* (North, 1990; 1993). North's action theory is also consistent with Asplund's motivation theory (ref. Asplund's motivation theory).

Primary task. An organization's primary task is what the system is designed to do.

Proposition. This is an overarching hypothesis. It says something about the relationship between several variables. A proposition relates to a hypothesis in the same way the main research problem relates to research

---

[7] North's action theory is a term we use here based on North's research.

questions.

Punctuation. By punctuation (Bateson, 1972:292-293) a distinction is drawn between cause and effect; this is done with a clear motive in mind. A causality is thus created which does not actually exist in the real world, and one is then free to discuss the effects of this cause which has been created through a process of punctuation.

A sequence of a process is selected, and then bracketed. In this way, we de-limit what is punctuated from the rest of the process. Figuratively, we may imagine this as a circle that is divided into small pieces; one piece of the circle is then selected and folded out into a straight line. This results in the creation of an artificial beginning and end. This beginning and end of course cannot exist in a circle, but only through the process of punctuation.

Social laws. Social laws constitute a pattern of a unique type. They are systemic and connected to a system of knowledge, and cannot change without the facts they represent also being changed (Bunge, 1983; 1983a). The main differences between a statement of a law and other statements are:

1. Law statements are general.

2. Law statements are systemic, i.e. they are related to the established system of knowledge.

3. Law statements have been verified through many studies.

A pattern may be understood as variables that are stable over a specific period of time. A social law is created when an observer gains insight into the pattern. By gaining such insight, we can also predict parts of behaviour or at least develop a rough estimate within a short period of time.

Social laws are further related to specific social systems, both in time and space. However, this does not represent any objection to social laws, because this is also true of natural laws (although these have a longer time span and are of a more general nature).

Social mechanism. Robert Merton (1967) brought the notion of social mechanisms into sociology, although we can find rudiments of this in both Weber – with the Protestant ethic as an explanation for the emergence of capitalism in Europe – and in Durkheim, who uses society as an explanation for a rising suicide rate. For Merton, social mechanisms are the building blocks of *middle range theories*. He defines social mechanisms as *social processes having designated consequences for designated parts of the social structure* (Merton, 1968:43). In the 1980s and 1990s, Jon Elster developed a new notion of the role of social mechanisms in sociology (Elster, 1983;1989). Hedstrom and Swedberg write that, *the advancement of social theory calls for an analytical approach that systematically seeks to explicate the social mechanisms that generate and explain observed associations between events* (Hedstrøm & Swedberg, 1998:1).

It is one thing to point out connections between phenomena. It is something quite different to point out satisfactory explanations for these relationships, which is what social mechanisms accomplish. A social mechanism tells us what will happen, how it will happen and why it will happen (Bunge, 1967). Social mechanisms are primarily analytical constructs which cannot necessarily be observed; in other words, they are epistemological, not ontological. However, social mechanisms are observable in their consequences. An intention can be a social mechanism of action. We cannot observe an intention, but we can interpret it in light of the consequences manifested through an action. Preferences can also function as a social mechanism for economic behaviour. We cannot observe a person's preferences, but we can interpret them in the light of the behavioural consequences that manifest themselves. Social mechanisms are, understood in this way, analytical constructs, indicating connections between events (Hernes, 1998).

Bunge says: "... *a social mechanism is a process in a concrete system, such that it is capable of being about or preventing some change in the system as a whole or in some of its subsystems*" (Bunge, 1997:414). By 'social mechanism' here we mean those activities that promote/inhibit social processes in relation to a specific problem / phenomenon.

Material resources and technology are social mechanisms of the economic subsystem; power is a social mechanism of the political subsystem; fundamental norms and values are a social mechanism of the cultural subsystem; and human relationships are a social mechanism of the social subsystem. These system-specific social mechanisms interact with each other to achieve certain goals, maintain these systems, or to avoid certain undesirable conditions in the system or the outside world.

The difficulty of discovering social mechanisms and distinguishing them from processes may be partly explained by the fact that social mechanisms are also processes (Bunge, 1997:414). For the application of social mechanisms, see the Boudon-Coleman diagram.

Social system. From a systemic perspective, social systems can be conceptual or concrete. Theories and analytical models are examples of conceptual systems. Further, social systems are *composed of people and their artifacts* (Bunge, 1996:21). Social systems are held together (in systemic reasoning) by **dynamic social relations** (such as emotions, interpretations, norms, etc.) and **social actions** (such as, cooperation, solidarity, conflict and communication, etc.). None of the social actions have precedence in the systemic interpretation of social systems, such as conflict in the case of Marx, and solidarity in the case of Durkheim.

Staccato-behaviour (erratic behaviour). If organizations introduce too many change processes in succession too quickly, a phenomenon may occur called "staccato-behaviour".

If an organization does not deal with this appropriately, it seems reasonable to assume that workers will become tired, burnt-out and de-motivated. Perhaps most damaging to business, employees will lose focus on their primary task - what the business is designed to do. In addition, businesses will often experience that this leads to an increasing degree of opportunistic behaviour (Ulrich, 2013a:260).

Strategic HR management. Strategic HR management is defined in this book as: *The choices an HR department makes with regard to human resources for the purposes of achieving the organization's goals.* This is analogous to the view of Storey et al. (2009:3) and consistent with the definition we employ of HR management. This means that strategic HR management must be focused on the *micro, meso* and *macro-levels*.

There are many definitions of strategic HR management. For instance, *use of human resources in order to achieve lasting competitive advantages for the business* (Mathis and Jackson, 2008:36); *management of the employees, expressed through management philosophy, policy and praxis* (Torrington et al., 2005:28); *development of a consistent practices in order to support the strategic goals of the business* (Mello, 2006:152); *a complex system with the following characteristics: vertical integration, horizontal integration, efficiency, partnership* (Schuler and Jackson, 2005).

Systemic thinking. Systemic thinking makes a distinction between the epistemological sphere (Bunge, 1985), the ontological sphere (Bunge, 1983), the axiological sphere (Bunge, 1989, 1996) and the ethical sphere (Bunge, 1989). Systemic thinking makes a clear distinction between intention and behaviour. Intention is something that should be *understood*, while behaviour is something that should be *explained*. To understand an intention we must study the historical factors, situations and contexts, as well as the expectation mechanisms. Behaviour must be explained with respect to the context, relationships and situation it unfolds in. What implication does the distinction between intention and behavior have for the study of social systems?

Interpretation of meaning is an important part of the *intention aspect* in the distinction. Explanation and prediction become an essential part of the *behavioral aspect* of the distinction.

In systemic thinking it is the link between the interpretation of meaning and explanation, and prediction, which provides historical and social sciences with practical strength. By making a distinction between intention and behaviour, the historical and the social sciences are interpretive, explanatory and predictive projects. According to systemic thinking, many of the contradictions in the historical and social sciences spring from the fact that a distinction is not made between intention and behaviour. The problem of the historical and social sciences is that the actors who are studied have both intentions and they also exercise types of behaviour; however, this isn't problematic as long as we make a distinction between intention and behaviour. By simultaneously introducing the distinction between intention and behaviour, systemic thinking has made it possible to identify, for instance, partial explanations from each of two main epistemological positions, namely, the naturalists and anti-naturalists (Johannessen & Olaisen, 2005; 2006), and synthesize these explanations into new knowledge.

Systemic thinking emphasizes circular causal processes, also called *interactive causal processes*, in addition to linear causal processes (Johannessen, 1996; 1997). Systemic thinking argues that to understand objective social facts, one must examine the subjective aspects of these. In systemic thinking, objective social facts exist, but they are often more difficult to grasp than facts in the natural world, because social facts are often influenced by expectations, emotions, prejudices, ideology and economic and social interests. *"Aspect-seeing"* is thus a way of approaching these social facts.

Emergents are central to systemic thinking. A pattern behind the problem or phenomenon is always sought in systemic investigations.

Patterns may be revealed by studying the underlying processes that constitute a phenomenon or problem, *and the search for pattern is what scientific research is all about* (Bunge, 1996:42).

According to systemic thinking it is a misconception to say that the facts are social constructions. The misunderstanding involves confusing our *concepts* concerning facts and our *hypotheses* about the facts together with the facts. Our concepts and hypotheses are mental constructs. The facts, however, are not mental constructs. Social need, for instance, is not a social fact; it is a mental construct of, for instance, starvation. Starvation is a social fact. Social need is a mental or social construction. Not being able to read is a social fact. Illiteracy is, however, a social construction.

A *symbol* should symbolize something, just as a *concept* should delineate something. A *hypothesis* should explain something or express something about relationships. A conceptual *model* should say something about the relationships between concepts. A *theory* should say something about relationships between propositions. Physical or social facts are untouched by all these mental constructions. That one can through constructs change social facts, or that social facts are changed as a social consequence of using constructs, is neither original nor new.

The aim of theoretical research, according to the systemic position, is the construction of systems, i.e. theories (Bunge, 1974: v). The order in systemic research is thus: Theory - Analysis - Synthesis.

In the methodological sphere, the systemic position has its main focus on relationships, both in terms of concrete things, ideas and knowledge. Consequently, systemic thinking encourages interdisciplinary and multidisciplinary approaches to problems or phenomena.

The systemic position thus attempts to bridge the gap between methodological individualism and methodological collectivism, which is considered the classic controversy in historical- and social sciences.

The perceptions that an observer has about social systems will influence his/her actions, regardless of whether the perceptions are true or fallacious. Systemic investigations start, therefore, writes Bunge *from individuals embedded in a society that preexists them and watch how their actions affect society and alter it* (Bunge, 1996:241). The study of social systems from a systemic perspective for these reasons always includes the triad: actors - observers - social systems.

The observer tries to uncover a system's composition, environment and structure. Then the actors' subjective perception of composition, environment and structure are examined. In other words, both the subjective and objective aspects are studied. When we wish to study changes in social systems, from a systemic point of view, we have to examine the social mechanisms (drivers) that influence changes; both internal and external social mechanisms must be identified. This study takes place within the four subsystems: the economic, political, cultural and relational. According to systemic thinking, social changes occur along seven axes:

1. As an *expectation* of new relationships, values, power constellations, technologies and distribution of material resources.

2. As a result of our *beliefs* (mental models) about relationships, values, power constellations, technical and material resources.

3. As a result of *psychological elements*, such as: irritation, crisis, discomfort, unsatisfactory life, unworthy life, loss of well-being, etc.

4. As a result of *communication* in and between systems.

5. As a result of an *understanding of connections* (contextual understanding).

6. As a result of learning and new *self-knowledge*.

7. As a result of *new ideas* and ways of thinking.

Historiography, from a systemic perspective, has one clear goal: to investigate what happened, where it happened, when it happened, how it happened, why it happened, and with what results.

Systemic assumptions related to historiography and social sciences may be expressed in the following (Bunge 1998:263):

a. The past has existed.
b. Parts of the past can be known.
c. Every uncovering of the past will be incomplete.
d. New data, techniques, and systemizations and structuring will reveal new aspects of the past.
e. Historical knowledge is developed through new data, discoveries, hypotheses and approaches.

In systemic thinking if changes are to take place, then the material will sometimes be given precedence; at other times, ideology, ideas and thinking are given precedence. In other contexts, there is a systemic link between the material and ideas that is needed to bring about changes. In such contexts, it is difficult and irrelevant to say what is the primary driver, i.e. the material or ideas; this would be on par with discussing what came first, the chicken or the egg.

The processes that drive social change, according to a systemic perspective, are the interaction between the economic, political, relational and cultural subsystems. In some situations, one of these four perspectives will prevail, whereas in others it will be one or more of the four subsystems that are the drivers of social change. In many cases, it is precisely the interaction between the four subsystems that leads to social changes.

In this context the systemic perspective may be described by saying that material conditions/energy, such as economic relationships, may provide the ground from which ideologies develop, but that these ideologies in return influence the development of the material. Whether material conditions / energy or ideology comes first is often determined by a historiographical punctuation process (Bateson, 1972:163).

The systemic perspective balances historical materialism and historical idealism. It assumes that overall social changes are the result of economic, political, social and cultural factors, in addition to the interaction between material conditions / energy and ideas. Furthermore, a systemic perspective views any society as being interwoven into its surroundings (Bunge, 1998: 275). When a historian considers a historical situation – such as the massacre in Van in April 1915 – from this perspective then he is trying *to throw light upon the internal working of a past culture and society* (Stone, 1979: 19).

The systemic position attempts to view the relevant event in a larger context, in order to find *the patterns which combine* (Bateson, 1972:273-274), because *change depends upon feedback loop* (Bateson, 1972:274). Bunge says about this position: *By placing the particular in a sequence, adopting a broad perspective the systemist overcomes the idiographic/nomothetic duality, ..., as well as the concomitant narrative/structural opposition* (Bunge 1998:275). This means, metaphorically, that the systemic researcher uses a microscope, telescope and a helicopter to investigate patterns over time.

Systemic research strategy is a *zig-zagging between the micro-meso and macro levels* (Bunge, 1998:277). Through a systemic research strategy the researcher has ample opportunities to use a Boudon-Coleman diagram.

Systemic thinking examines four types of changes[8].

Type I change concerns individuals who change history, such as Genghis Khan, Hitler, Stalin, Mao Zedong, etc.

Type II change concerns groups of people acting together who change history. Examples of Type II change include the invasion of the Roman Empire by peoples from the north; and the Ottoman expansion into the Balkans between the late 1400s and when the Ottoman Empire was pushed back partly due to nationalist liberation movements in the early 1900s.

Type III change include changes in history that are caused by natural disasters, such as the volcanic eruption that destroyed Pompeii. Climate change may also be said to an example of a type III change.

Type IV change involves a total change in the way of thinking, such as the emergence of new religions, like Islam, or a new political ideology, such as Marxism.

The systemic researcher attempts to explore the relationship between the four types of changes. A single event is in itself not necessarily of special

---

[8] The four types of changes are related to Bateson's (1972:279-309) work on different types of learning, especially those discussed in his chapter *Logical types of learning and communication*.

interest to the systemic researcher; rather, the focus is on the *system of events* of which the single event is a part.

All the social sciences are used in the systemic position to seek insight, understanding and to explain a phenomenon or problem.

Tacit knowledge. Knowledge that is difficult to communicate to others as information. It is also very difficult, if at all possible, to digitize.

The knowledge-based perspective. The knowledge-based perspective is defined here as creating, expanding and modifying internal and external competencies to promote what the organization is designed to do (Grant, 2003: 203).

The resource-based perspective. This perspective can be defined as the structuring and systematization of the organization's internal *resources* so it is difficult for competitors to copy them.

Theory. Here understood as a system of propositions (Bunge, 1974: v).

Index

A

abstract, 91
agility, 7
ambiguity, 51, 56
analysis, 20, 21, 99, 130, 132, 145, 169, 182
assumptions, 29, 38, 109, 138, 154, 198
autonomy, 77
autopoiesis theory, 105, 108, 112, 151, 156
autopoietic, 12, 106, 108, 110, 111, 112, 124, 131, 158

B

boundaries, 66, 80, 130, 135, 136, 138, 139

C

change, 6, 13, 14, 18, 27, 32, 35, 37, 54, 63, 77, 84, 92, 93, 95, 98, 99, 103, 106, 113, 120, 122, 134, 135, 137, 138, 148, 162, 169, 170, 172, 173, 175, 178, 180, 187, 190, 191, 195, 199, 200, 201
clusters, 59, 66, 67, 68, 69, 70, 71, 72, 73, 75, 77, 79, 86, 87, 89, 91, 177
co-creation, 58, 67, 72, 74, 75, 76, 171
cognitive openness, 12, 107, 110, 115
communication, 6, 13, 16, 38, 63, 70, 87, 105, 110, 111, 116, 130, 131, 132, 133, 134, 135, 136, 138, 153, 171, 191, 197, 201
complexity, 69, 77, 92, 93, 127
conceptualisation, 79
co-operation, 37, 54, 58, 74, 75, 76, 77, 82, 138
creative, 9, 11, 12, 14, 59, 62, 65, 68, 70, 72, 75, 79, 81, 82, 84, 85, 106, 140, 148, 177, 183, 184
creative energy, 59, 79, 81, 82
creative tension, 12, 14
customers, 14, 16, 30, 61, 81, 172, 176

D

discontinuity, 56
disposition, 13, 26
distributed, 68, 73, 80, 81, 84, 86, 87, 89, 90, 185
dynamics, 28, 42, 91, 95, 159

E

emergent, 93, 94, 108, 174, 177
emerges, 90, 174
expectations, 63, 64, 81, 86, 109, 111, 113, 114, 116, 117, 126, 127, 128, 129, 137, 153, 175, 194
expertise, 27, 59, 60, 62, 66, 67, 68, 70, 71, 72, 73, 74, 75, 76, 77, 79, 80, 81, 84, 86, 87, 88, 89, 91, 173, 176
Explicit knowledge, 24, 64, 104, 173

F

Feed-forward, 175
foresight, 14, 78, 100
fragmented, 81, 89, 185

G

generalisation, 79
global, 57, 58, 59, 61, 63, 66, 68, 69, 70, 71, 72, 73, 75, 77, 78, 79, 80, 81, 83, 84, 85, 86, 87, 88, 91, 94, 148, 166, 176, 177, 180, 182, 185
Global clusters, 70, 72

H

habitat, 80, 81
habitus, 116, 117
Hidden knowledge, 26, 29, 65, 104, 178
hierarchical, 69, 125
high-tech, 59, 67, 68, 69, 72, 73, 74, 77, 85, 86, 88, 90, 91, 184
hypercompetition., 27

I

imitation, 9, 51, 143, 148
immanent, 92
information, 6, 8, 9, 11, 12, 16, 24, 25, 30, 31, 36, 38, 39, 41, 43, 53, 56, 65, 70, 78, 80, 85, 87, 93, 104, 106, 108, 109, 111, 114, 116, 126, 127, 131, 132, 140, 142, 152, 168, 173, 176, 181, 182, 183, 202
Information capital, 125
info-structure, 70
infrastructure, 70, 182
innovation, iv, v, 6, 7, 9, 10, 11, 12, 13, 15, 17, 19, 20, 22, 28, 29, 31, 32, 33, 35, 36, 37,

38, 39, 40, 41, 42, 43, 44, 45, 46, 47, 51, 53, 56, 57, 63, 64, 65, 66, 68, 73, 75, 76, 77, 80, 81, 84, 86, 87, 88, 91, 94, 95, 97, 101, 107, 111, 114, 121, 127, 130, 132, 136, 137, 138, 142, 143, 145, 146, 147, 148, 150, 151, 152, 153, 154, 156, 160, 161, 166, 170, 171, 172, 173, 177, 178, 180, 182, 185, 207
innovation-driven economy, 88
innovations, iv, 36, 38, 57, 59, 64, 71, 74, 75, 77, 89, 101, 121, 147, 148, 149, 150, 166, 168, 172, 178
institutions, 6, 12, 117, 120, 124, 164
integration, 6, 26, 31, 53, 61, 66, 67, 75, 152, 177, 192
interaction, 29, 65, 66, 106, 124, 125, 126, 131, 132, 133, 135, 137, 147, 169, 199
interpretation, 24, 79, 191, 193
inventions, 36

K

knowledge creation, 6, 11, 12, 17, 21, 22, 49, 151
knowledge development, 8, 37, 66
knowledge economy, 58, 59, 61, 63, 66, 87, 88, 91, 94, 97, 100, 166, 176, 185
knowledge integration, 8, 22, 31, 37, 43, 61, 74, 151
knowledge management, 6, 35, 39, 97, 180
knowledge workers, 7, 8, 22, 32, 33, 34, 68, 77, 84, 85, 184
knowledge-based company, 16, 17
knowledge-integration, 11

L

Lego organisations, 87, 88

M

management, iv, v, 7, 8, 11, 13, 17, 30, 32, 35, 38, 39, 54, 57, 65, 76, 95, 105, 161, 166, 179, 182, 185, 192, 207
Merton, 188, 189
metaphor, 14, 25, 90
middle managers, 18

N

norm, 109, 115, 123
normative basis, 36, 107, 109, 110, 113, 114, 115, 116, 117, 118, 119, 121, 124, 125, 130, 135, 136, 153, 154, 155
normative closure, 110, 111, 135
normative superstructure, 106, 107, 113, 114, 116, 118, 120, 121, 123, 124, 125, 129, 155